AFTER LIVES

AFTER LIVES

On Biography and the Mysteries
of the Human Heart

Megan Marshall

MARINER BOOKS
New York Boston

FIRST EDITION

Designed by Emily Snyder

Library of Congress Cataloging-in-Publication Data has been applied for.

ISBN 978-0-618-68418-2

24 25 26 27 28 LBC 5 4 3 2 1

For my grandchildren

We go out of life with the same passionate eagerness to enter into the lives of others and to understand them that we brought into it.

—GAMALIEL BRADFORD,
Biography and the Human Heart

CONTENTS

Introduction: Vital Documents

THE MANILA FILE FOLDER LABELED "Vital Documents" traveled with me from dorm room to off-campus apartment in my student days, then through a succession of residences as I moved in with my college boyfriend, married, raised children, divorced, and fell in love again. Filed under "V" in the depths of a two-drawer cabinet, the folder—really a paper pouch with closed sides—still holds my birth certificate and Social Security card, my first passport, acquired for a European honeymoon in 1980, and three later ones. My marriage certificate entered the folder along with that first passport, to be joined in the years ahead by two daughters' birth certificates, their passports, and a lock of dark blond hair from my oldest's first haircut.

I always knew what was in my "Vital Documents" file and where to find it. But I rarely removed the paper pouch from the cabinet, simply rummaged around in its contents to pull out what was needed. Until the day I got curious about my four passport photos. I'd just finished writing a biography of Elizabeth Bishop, my poetry teacher at Harvard in the 1970s, and while researching the book I'd been mesmerized by the miniature portraits in her half dozen passports preserved in the Bishop archive at her alma mater, Vassar College.

Bishop made her first trip to Europe in her mid-twenties too. There she was, frozen in time back in 1935—demur, lip-sticked, apprehensive, yet with the hint of a smile. I knew what she couldn't, that she was between tragedies: the recent, sordid death of her mother, who'd been confined in a mental institution for nearly two decades; the soon-to-come car crash in the French countryside that severed the right arm of her best friend and traveling companion, Margaret Miller, an artist who would never paint again. Bishop hadn't been driving the car, but she was already a binge drinker. A lifelong asthmatic, she struggled mightily against both afflictions with little success. The poet appeared grim and even haggard in the later photographs, the last one taken for a trip to Greece five months before she died of a cerebral aneurysm at age sixty-eight in 1979. I marveled at the contrast between those fixed, joyless expressions and the delight, the release from her demons, I knew she'd experienced in the travel her passports enabled; I'd found a red poppy pressed between the pages of the diary she kept on the Greek island cruise with her much younger lover, Alice Methfessel.

I wanted to see what I could learn from my own passport photos, and I pulled out the entire folder, only to find that Elizabeth Bishop was there too. Scribbled in black felt-tip were instructions I still remember as uttered in my professor's distinctive voice—a low Nova Scotian burr with a Vassar finish—jotted down on the front panel of a file that must have commenced its long life as my repository for that semester's class notes and drafts. She'd given us directions from Harvard Square to her condo on a remote pier in Boston's North End: "sub. to Haymarket, Hanover, down Fleet, black building, called Lewis Wharf, facing water, #437." And a date and time: "Wed. Jan. 12th—7:30." We'd been invited to a party—her first-ever semester's end celebration, I'd learn in researching her life, the finale to her last-ever poetry workshop. She would be dead two years later.

But that night, dressed casually in slacks and soft white cardigan instead of the usual tweed suit that seemed only to increase her discomfort at the head of the workshop table, our diminutive white-haired professor sipped wine, chatted, and smiled, radiant as she'd never been in class. Now I was the one to feel ill at ease, far from campus, among Miss Bishop's poet friends: bearded men in V-neck sweaters invited to join our crew. We sat in a circle of chairs in the living room—exposed brick, dark windows on Boston Harbor—and listened to the poets read their own *real* poetry, listened to Miss Bishop read "One Art," her best-known poem, then still new: "The art of losing isn't hard to master. . . ."

My scrawled directions to 437 Lewis Wharf brought it all back. I had thought I wanted to be a poet, but I'd never seen a poet outside a classroom or an auditorium—and now here I was, in a poet's home. Absorbed by the scene around me, I was suddenly and painfully aware that all I knew of Miss Bishop and the other eminent writers I'd been fortunate to learn from were the workshop witticisms and possibly forced expressions of interest required by their teaching jobs. My fledgling efforts on the page melted into insignificance, even as my longing to join their number flickered inside me.

I didn't become a poet, but the night among poets helped to make me a different kind of writer: a biographer. The oddly seductive feeling of proximate distance—captivated by my host, yet apart, not one of *them*—was my initiation to the biographer's role. I'd been a fly on the wall at a consequential moment in literary history. Elizabeth Bishop's reputation rose steadily after her death, in no small part due to "One Art," the poem she read to us that evening; she is now often named one of the most influential American poets of the twentieth century. Frank Bidart, one of the acolytes present, went on to win nearly every prize available to a poet. Bishop's lover, Alice Methfessel, also in attendance, would be revealed as the impetus for "One Art" and its meditation on loss.

I wouldn't write about Bishop yet. The thought never occurred to me back then. First I had to earn my place in New England, the region I'd fled to from sunbaked Southern California in search of an intellectual home—but which, as I settled into the reading rooms of libraries and historical societies with my portable typewriter and made friends with archivists and other scholars, grew to be more than that. For nearly three decades I researched and wrote about four nineteenth-century heroines whose formative years were lived mostly in cities and towns within the circle of I-495, Boston's expansive ring road. By the time I'd published *The Peabody Sisters: Three Women Who Ignited American Romanticism* in 2005 and *Margaret Fuller: A New American Life* in 2013, most people who knew me assumed I was a "born-and-bred" New Englander. The famously frosty native Bay Staters I'd lived among for so long turned to me for insights on their heritage.

The literary scholar and biographer Paul Murray Kendall has written that "any biography uneasily shelters an autobiography within it," and I won't deny that my work on the three Peabody women and Margaret Fuller sometimes felt like self-exploration. I'd grown up attending a permissive Unitarian Sunday school in a city whose population trended toward the Evangelical. I identified with the pint-sized Unitarian Elizabeth Peabody, who provoked theological disputes with her orthodox schoolmates at a time when the denomination was brand new, and I learned from her diaries and letters the history of my family's religion. I drew on my experience as a middle child to intuit the feelings of Mary Peabody as she sought to differentiate herself from her powerfully passionate older and younger sisters while keeping the peace. At thirty-six, Mary married the politician and educator Horace Mann, and on days when I finished transcribing one of her spidery handwritten letters and typed out her new signature— "M.M."—well, I remembered Kendall's further advisory: "On the trail of another man, the biographer must put up with finding himself at every turn."

By the time I was ready to write Elizabeth Bishop's life, nearly forty years had passed since the class party. I'd grown impatient with the conventions of literary biography, especially the imperative on the biographer's part to remain out of sight. I'd always aspired to meet the standard set by Leon Edel, whose five-volume life of Henry James dominated the field when I started out: "The biographer truly succeeds if a distinct literary form can be found for the particular life." I wrote about the Peabodys and Margaret Fuller in novelistic style, finding the narrative arc best suited to the facts of their lives. I decided to bring memoir into my third book. I had known Elizabeth Bishop. How could I stay out of it? Indeed, this seemed the only way to establish objectivity, a proximate distance readers could trust. I would separate our intersecting stories, allow them to run in parallel as alternating chapters, until at last they met in the final years of Bishop's life, the beginning of mine as a writer. The moments when I "found myself" on the trail of Elizabeth Bishop—those occasional eerie coincidences that I stumbled upon in the course of research—would be revealed in this way as well. I'd be showing my work.

If I'd pulled out my "Vital Documents" folder while writing the book, I'd have included that moment too. When I extracted my first passport photo from the file, I wasn't surprised to see myself clad in white collar and dark jacket, just like Elizabeth Bishop in her photo taken at the same age, and holding back a smile. But instead, the visual echo and the chance emergence of the repurposed folder primed me for the essays I began to write soon after the publication of *Elizabeth Bishop: A Miracle for Breakfast* in 2017. I'd entered a period I've come to think of as A.L.—"After Lives"—when the loose ends of the full-scale narratives I'd researched teased my imagination, and the documents of my own history, piled up in closets over the years, called out for exploration. I'd turned my back on my Californian upbringing to become a New Englander—or at least a writer about New England. It was time to close the gap.

It was also a time when the shock of my late partner Scott Harney's final illness and death, which played out against a backdrop of national unrest and worldwide mourning, spurred me to write in shorter bursts, as if in rhythm with the evolving states of emergency. In 2018, I read my grandparents' letters written from

Paris one hundred years earlier to learn what it had been like to live through a global crisis—World War I. In 2020, I reflected on my private experience of loss as the world grieved the hundreds of thousands dead in the first wave of the COVID-19 pandemic. A year later, the fiftieth reunion of my high school class prompted me to revisit the tragic death in 1970 of our seventeen-year-old schoolmate Jonathan Jackson, gunned down in a failed attempt to free his older brother, George, from prison. Later essays burrowed deeper into my past and purpose as a biographer as I worked to regain my balance as a writer, living alone for the first time in a new era of ominous portents.

"Every living human being is a biographer from childhood," wrote the early twentieth-century biographer Gamaliel Bradford. He had in mind the way, as children, we endlessly observe our siblings and elders, compare ourselves with them, and find inspiration or take warning. But a child who grows up to become a biographer is a special case. Observation, evaluation, and inference become tricks of the trade. In writing about her own life, the biographer also seeks proximate distance: She checks her memory against verifiable facts, interviews witnesses, examines documents, establishes context, aims for a cultural history of the self. All this I have tried to do in the six chapters of *After Lives*.

Yet as the biographer knows better than anyone, there are memories that can't be verified, questions that can't be answered. When did I empty the file folder of my student work and affix the penciled-in label "Vital Documents"? I have no recollection. And how I wish I still had the poems I'd written under Elizabeth Bishop's guidance, amateurish and insignificant as they would appear to anyone else today. They bore my notes on her comments in class, evidence that I'd once mattered to her, if only briefly as one in a succession of students eager for her approval. What was most vital about the file was not the passports and certificates it still held, but the container itself and its long-forgotten message: You were there. It's the message from the past we all crave and, for those of us blessed with historical imaginations, just a heartbeat away from the sensation biography at its best aims to convey: You *are* there.

AFTER LIVES

*D*EAD MEN TELL NO TALES. But dead women do—at least to me. They speak in questions. Una Hawthorne—the eldest child of Nathaniel and Sophia Hawthorne, whose puckish disposition as a girl had been grafted by her father onto little Pearl, Hester Prynne's willful out-of-wedlock daughter in *The Scarlet Letter*—was the first and most insistent. Una would not let me go.

I'd given two decades to researching and writing a biography of the Peabody sisters, the youngest of whom was Nathaniel's wife, Sophia, a promising artist at the time of their wedding in 1842, active in her studio through their first year of marriage. That's where my book ended, with Una's birth in 1844, the year Sophia turned thirty-five and Nathaniel, forty. By then the Hawthornes and Sophia's two sisters, Elizabeth and Mary, were well launched, along with the bold intellectual and social movement—transcendentalism—they'd done so much to initiate. As an aspiring writer who struggled to make time for my work while raising two daughters, I'd been reluctant to face Sophia's renunciation of her talent in motherhood, her decision, as she once wrote to a wealthy friend who'd offered to pay for a nanny after the birth of Una's baby sister, Rose, Sophia's third and last child, so she might return to her easel: "painting—for the present must go by the board—& what is more, shall go." Her children would be "the best pictures I ever painted." Sophia Hawthorne never completed, or even commenced, another work of art.

Now, on a warm evening in late June 2006, a year after my book was published, I was facing both mother and daughter in death. The Dominican Sisters of Hawthorne, New York, an order of Catholic nuns founded by Rose, who'd taken vows in midlife, had arranged for the transfer of Sophia's and Una's remains from Kensal Green Cemetery in London, where they'd been buried in 1871 and 1877—Sophia at sixty-one, Una at thirty-three. The two women were to be "reunited" with Nathaniel, as the Dominican Sisters thought of it, on Authors Ridge in Sleepy Hollow Cemetery, a popular tourist site in Concord, Massachusetts, where the town's famous literary families were interred: the Emersons, Thoreaus, Alcotts, and Nathaniel Hawthorne, whose wife and children had died too far off to keep him company in the afterlife.

We were seated on folding chairs in a small, windowless assembly room at the interior of Rosary Hill Home, the hospice for impoverished cancer patients Rose had established in 1900 and the Dominican Sisters still operated, Sophia and Una's first stop on their way home to Concord. Sister Mary Joseph, the Dominican Sisters' public relations officer, had invited me and a fifth-generation representative of the Hawthorne family, the poet Alison Deming, to witness the Hawthorne women's return to the United States. A plain wooden casket—child-sized, Sister Mary Joseph said—lay before us on a table. She slipped out of the room, the white skirts of her habit rustling as she shut the door, telling us, "You can look inside if you'd like. But you won't find much, just bits of bone and cloth. It's been a long time." More than 120 years.

Raised Unitarian in a family that prefers cremation and long-delayed "celebrations of life" for our dead, I'd never attended a wake or viewing, the ritual I assumed Sister Mary Joseph was permitting us to enact in private. The undeniable curiosity I felt was mixed with dread, despite the assurance there would be no skeletons. I deferred to Alison, the blood relative. She lifted the lid.

Tissue paper lined the box, and there were layers separated by more tissue paper that I knew we wouldn't explore. But on top rested a few fragments of bone, slim and white, like worn-down bars of soap; the remnant of a pale blue knit stocking; a tarnished silver Maltese cross. And two full heads of hair, each culminating in a long, thick ropelike braid. Sophia's was salt-and-pepper gray, Una's the auburn of the pastel portrait done three years before her death that I'd seen on the wall at the Concord Free Public Library. In the portrait Una's braid was coiled neatly around her head; her hair shimmered, safely two-dimensional, behind glass. Here the strands were a deep rusty red, and real.

It took a few days—beyond the next morning's solemn procession in the cemetery, the touching remarks of more Hawthorne descendants at graveside, the speeches for the public under a tent on the grounds of the Old Manse where Una was born so long ago in early spring, "a third spirit [linked] forever to our own,"

Nathaniel had written to Sophia: "Is she not thine and mine, the symbol of the one true union in the world, and of our love in Paradise?"—to realize what had puzzled and disturbed me as I peered into the coffin. What I'd seen wasn't supposed to be. I should have found one braid of gray and one of white.

IN A 1978 essay, the literary critic Elizabeth Hardwick, who was leery of biography although she would go on to write one herself on Herman Melville, complained of the way historical figures are "fixed by the glue of biography." She was referring to the living movie star Faye Dunaway; Hardwick argued that film actors succeed by establishing a trademark look that, "once imprinted upon the mind . . . refuses to change its meaning" from one role to the next. "It is the star cast in stone we go to see again and again." In Hardwick's view, the biographer's goal is the same, to sculpt a fixed persona that remains consistent and easily recognizable through the narrative. By the end of the book, the biographer has cast her pliant, real-life subject in stone, fixed her in amber—or glue.

Few biographers I know would agree. They might have closed the book on their subject, reluctantly or with relief, but the spirit lingers, untethered and tempting: in transcriptions of letters and journals we'd still like to quote stored away in file folders we can't bear to toss; in inspirational messages tacked to bulletin boards that continue to fire us up; in photos hanging on our office walls that won't stop staring at us expectantly. The relationship endures, even if we go on to write about someone else. The late James Atlas, whose first biography of the poet Delmore Schwartz

was written before the internet age, chose Saul Bellow for his next
book. The project carried him into the digital era when, Atlas
once told me, his password on secure websites and at ATMs was
always some variation on "Delmore."

The character we've come to know almost like a family member is hardly static; the curiosity that drove us to examine a life so
rigorously we could fill hundreds of pages with its facts just won't
quit. New information comes our way from knowledgeable readers, or we may seek it out. A biographer of Margaret Fuller from
the 1990s, Joan von Mehren, couldn't stop puzzling over the mystery that had eluded Fuller's biographers, not to mention her
grieving family members and friends, ever since the pioneering
feminist died at age forty in a shipwreck: Had she actually married the young Italian nobleman who fathered her child? All three
drowned in the wreck off Fire Island, and Fuller had never described a wedding or given a date in the letters she began to write
home confessing the secret love affair she'd carried on during the
two years she lived in Rome reporting on the Italian revolution
of 1848–49 for Horace Greeley's *New-York Tribune*. When she
decided to bring her family back to America in 1850, she simply
announced she was married and began to use a new name.

But was she truly Margaret Fuller, Marchesa d'Ossoli? Fuller's first biographers concocted their own story to protect her
reputation from posthumous scandal, with a wedding date set just
before little Nino Ossoli's conception. Successive biographers
sifted the few shreds of evidence to offer a version that aligned
with their views of Fuller: yes, she'd married, at last finding
womanly fulfillment; no, she hadn't, adhering to her stated belief
that marriage is a "corrupt social contract." Finally, while verify-
ing Fuller's Roman addresses in an Italian archive devoted to real

estate transactions a few years after completing her own account, Joan von Mehren mentioned her frustration with the mystery to a fellow researcher, Roberto Colzi, a retired banker with an interest in Roman architecture. Now *his* curiosity was piqued. Leaving von Mehren to her project of developing an itinerary for a tour group of Fuller scholars, Colzi scoured numerous church archives and eventually retrieved a record of Nino's baptism, which clearly stated his parents were "coniugi," a married couple.

Questions remained: When did they marry? Might they have dissembled? But here at last was something to work with, and proof of Fuller's intent to make the connection legal. Future biographers could start their own investigations there.

———

UNA HAWTHORNE WAS calling to me. I'd ended my book with her birth, but I hadn't closed my mind to her presence in the sources I'd consulted while researching her parents' lives and reconstructing the love story that played a prominent role in my narrative—a romance that seemed surprisingly modern. The Hawthornes met after each had served a solitary apprenticeship of a decade or more in their profession. Nathaniel Hawthorne was among the first American writers of fiction to attempt to make a living by his pen; lack of a steady income was the reason for his three-year secret engagement to Sophia Peabody, the gifted painter who'd won his heart with a sketch of one of his characters. They didn't cohabit, as a pair of artists might today, but they considered themselves married from the date of their engagement and addressed each other in passionate love letters as husband and wife. When at last they planned a wedding in July

1842, Nathaniel joked that in performing the ceremony the minister would have to "thrust himself between" them.

The Hawthornes were older parents with a penchant for idealizing themselves and the Edenic surroundings into which their first child was born, a veritable "fairy-land" on the banks of the Concord River, "sheltered from the turmoil of life's ocean," in Nathaniel's terms. Sophia had suffered a miscarriage during an otherwise blissful honeymoon year, and she recorded the loss in words etched with the diamond on her wedding ring into a windowpane of the "moss-grown country parsonage" her husband dubbed the "Old Manse," rented out to them by their near neighbor Ralph Waldo Emerson: "Man's accidents are God's purposes." Una's arrival during the second year of their marriage must have been by divine intent.

Over the objections of friends, who worried the choice was "too imaginative," the couple adhered to a decision, made before the child's birth, to name her for the uncommonly virtuous heroine of Edmund Spenser's epic poem *The Faerie Queene*, the king's "onely daughter deare." Nathaniel agreed there was risk in selecting a name that "has never before been warmed with human life," but in her first weeks Una's living presence had given it "a natural warmth," her father claimed. He expected that "when she has worn it through her lifetime, and perhaps transmitted it to descendants of her own, this beautiful name will have become naturalized on earth;—whereby we shall have done a good deed in first bringing it out of the realm of Faery."

Yet the months after Una's birth brought hardship. Sophia nursed her baby and soon also another little girl born that year in Concord to Margaret Fuller's sister Ellen, whose breast milk failed. Nathaniel sold stories to magazines, but payment was minimal and erratic. By winter, Nathaniel's need for paying work in the form of a political appointment—ultimately, a customs-house job—drove the Hawthornes from their country retreat. They made plans to move to Salem and a house they'd share with Nathaniel's widowed mother and two unmarried sisters. There would be more Hawthorne children, but only Una had been born during "the calm summer of my heart and mind," as Nathaniel described the Old Manse years in the introduction to his collection of stories published after the move in hopes of recouping his losses. Sophia left behind a second inscription on a windowpane, marking the former rectory with an indelible image of Una's infant happiness. I read the delicate tracings myself on the day of the reinterment:

Una Hawthorne
stood on this window
sill January 22'd 1845
while the trees were all
glass chandeliers a goodly
show which she liked
much tho' only Ten
months old

Another vision of Una had stayed with me, from a book published in the 1950s by the Columbia professor Vernon Loggins called *The Hawthornes*. Loggins traced the genealogy of the family through seven generations, beginning with Nathaniel's colonial ancestors and ending with his daughters, Una and Rose, and their middle sibling, Julian. In the final chapters, Loggins described Una's death, a little over three decades after her auspicious birth. By then both Hawthorne parents were dead, and both Rose and Julian had married. Una herself was engaged to a writer of short stories, Albert Webster. While visiting Julian's family at their home on the outskirts of London, Una received word that the tubercular Webster had succumbed to illness on a ship bound for Hawaii, where he'd hoped to regain his health in advance of their wedding. During the next several months, Una's auburn hair "turned completely white," Loggins wrote, "and the least physical exertion caused fatigue." Una left Julian's house for a rest stay at an Anglican convent near Windsor where, within days, "she suddenly grew very weak. A message was sent to Julian, but before he arrived she was no more."

The story had always seemed improbable to me. Then, by chance, I'd seen Una's hair, and it was not white. Someone was lying.

————

I BEGAN SEARCHING for clues to what might have happened. How had the story of Una Hawthorne's extraordinary physical decline come into being, and—since I now knew the tale to be false in at least one significant particular—how had she died?

The first was easy to answer. Julian, who'd been summoned to Una's sickbed, offered it up in his own biography of his illustrious parents, the two-volume *Nathaniel Hawthorne and His Wife*. Why not believe him? He'd lived with Una during her last months, and he'd seen her in death, or so he said. One of the Clewer Sisters of the Community of St. John Baptist met him at the railroad station in Windsor: "We drove to the convent, and there, in the little cell-like room, on a narrow bed, she lay." In

Julian's version, Una's "dark auburn hair had become quite gray, and her vital functions and organs were (as the physician afterwards told me) those of an old woman." Loggins had merely improved on Julian's details, turning "quite gray" hair to the more dramatic "completely white." The dissembling began with Julian, the only family member to witness the scene. Yet as I turned to the records of the Hawthornes' family life, including two newly surfaced unpublished accounts of Una's last years, I had to wonder whether Julian was simply putting the finishing touches on a cover-up that had begun long before.

It was the little girl Una I knew best—indeed, millions of American high school graduates know her by proxy after reading *The Scarlet Letter* in English class. She may not have been the baby in Hester Prynne's arms as the novel's protagonist emerged from prison after serving her term for adultery in the book's opening chapter; that baby blinked and turned away from the bright sunlight after spending her first three months in a dungeon. But Una was there in the "elf-child" who danced through most of the following pages as Hester strove to keep the peace between the Reverend Arthur Dimmesdale, her secret lover who was Pearl's unacknowledged father, and the wizened alchemist Roger Chillingworth, Hester's long-lost husband, newly arrived in the Puritan village to take his vengeance.

Nathaniel's older sister, Elizabeth, who lived upstairs in the Hawthornes' Salem household as her brother wrote his first novel the year Una turned five, noticed the resemblance right away. Pearl was "unlike any other child, unless it be Una," she wrote after the book was published. Nathaniel's journals record impressions of Una that he transferred to his book. Like Pearl, when

Una played outdoors with neighborhood children, they "gaze at her with a kind of wonder—recognizing that she is not altogether like themselves." Like Pearl, Una displayed an uncanny know-ingness and a readiness to unsettle: "there is something that al-most frightens me about the child—I know not whether elfish or angelic, but, at all events, supernatural. She steps so boldly into the midst of everything, shrinks from nothing, has such a com-prehension of everything." Una was "a spirit strangely mingled with good and evil, haunting the house where I dwell." Was Una entering his novel, or was Nathaniel seeing Una as the character he'd imagined into being—the love child who could not be kept from asking unwelcome questions or speaking truths she intuited from the adults around her?

Or was Una just a normally inquisitive and unpredictable little girl whose father, unused to the ways of small children, was also a uniquely talented and ambitious writer? Whose mother channeled her own aesthetic passion into the dream of becoming a great man's helpmeet? Even as she'd honed her skills as a painter during her single years, Sophia Peabody harbored the private hope, set down in a poem in her diary titled "To the Unknown Yet Known," that she would someday find an artistic genius as her soul mate and devote herself to his welfare. It must have seemed to Sophia that Nathaniel Hawthorne had stepped right out of her poem. Strik-ingly handsome yet painfully shy, he'd published his first stories anonymously in periodicals; when a reviewer revealed his name in a favorable notice, Nathaniel was secretly pleased. He wrote in his journal, referring to the room in the family home in Salem where he'd sequestered himself to draft and redraft so many pages: "in this dismal and squalid chamber, FAME was won!" That was five years before his wedding and over a decade before *The Scarlet Letter* sold out its first printing in ten days, making him truly famous—and conferring on the Hawthorne children the dubious honor of becoming the offspring of an eminent man of letters, soon to be one of America's first celebrity authors.

A century later it would be a common story: aspiring writer seeks acclaim to assuage childhood deprivation—Nathaniel hardly knew his sea captain father, who died abroad when the boy was four; his mother withdrew in protracted mourning—only to offer his own children a perilous mix of pampering, heightened expectation, and neglect. But in the young America of the Hawthornes, Emersons, and Alcotts, child-rearing in a literary household was something new. During her early years, Una Hawthorne's parents moved the family four times in search of a suitable writing perch for her father, finally returning to Concord and a rambling farmhouse Nathaniel called the "Wayside" when she was eight years old. Nathaniel had written two more novels, increasing his fame but only scarcely his wealth. The once bold Una had begun to alarm her parents with an unaccountable lethargy or "premature ennui," in Nathaniel's description, and she spoke of wishing to "slip into God." His daughter suffered, the writer supposed, "from mere idleness and the want of a purpose in life." Should she be allowed to attend school, which might provide "a much happier childhood than . . . we can secure to her by a home-education"? The decision for now—and ultimately for all of Una's school years—was no. Sophia, who herself had never attended a school aside from those taught in the family home by her mother and older sister Elizabeth, was intent on crafting "the best pictures I ever painted."

THE HAWTHORNES MOVED to England in 1853, the same year
the suffragist Paulina Wright Davis began to publish America's
first woman's rights journal, *The Una*, adopting Spenser's intrepid princess as avatar for her "paper devoted to the elevation
of women." Nathaniel would serve as the American consul in the
bustling port at Liverpool, a lucrative political appointment he'd
earned by writing a campaign biography for his Bowdoin College
classmate, the newly elected president Franklin Pierce. Una was
nine, and her father sometimes teasingly called her "Onion"—
perhaps to win a smile from the daughter born of "the one true
union in the world," but also in recognition of the layers no one
could penetrate, Una's "rhinoceros-armor against sentiment or
tenderness." He decided that Una was, like himself, "more read-
ily awakened by fiction than realities." She loved to read.

Through four years in England and another two spent in Italy after Nathaniel's term as consul ended, the children's lessons
were supervised by Sophia and a succession of young govern-
esses. One of these described a typical parlor scene, with Nathaniel "ensconced in an easy chair in a meditating mood . . . his eyes
resting occasionally upon his lovely children as they pursued each
some favorite pastime,—Julian drawing shells for which he has
the greatest passion, Una reading Scott's poems and little Rose
flitting about among her toys, while Mrs. Hawthorne, the beautiful mother of the interesting group, reclined on the sofa with
the London papers." There were frequent outings, particularly in
Rome and Florence, to museums, parks, palaces, and cathedrals.
Both Julian and Rose became adept at sketching. A family album
includes Julian's portrait of a quite differently comported Una—
eyes fixed in a spectral gaze, hair released from its confining braid
and wildly askew—an image that may speak more truthfully

of Una than his published account of her demise. The undated sketch could have documented any of the several dark episodes of his older sister's young life.

At fifteen in Rome, Una contracted malaria and lingered near death for days, a brush with tragedy that brought the Hawthornes' Italian idyll to a close. At sixteen, shortly after the family returned to America, Una suffered a mental collapse. There is little record of what happened, aside from several letters written by Nathaniel from the Wayside in late September and early October 1860 to Franklin Pierce and his publisher, William D. Ticknor. "All the violent symptoms were allayed by the first application of electricity," he reported to Pierce, "and within two days she was in such a condition as to require no further restraint." An early form of electroshock therapy, "medical electricity," had succeeded in calming Una's "derangements," which the practitioner—"a certain electrical witch" or "doctress," he wrote to Ticknor, utilizing a "galvanic battery"—ascribed to "a liver-complaint and a slight affection of the heart, probably produced or strengthened by the Roman fever." Yet malaria—termed "Roman fever" by the English-speaking tourists who suffered from it—is not known to cause residual bouts of insanity. Nathaniel might not have written so openly to his friends of Una's case if he hadn't believed in the diagnosis and the promise of his daughter's "complete restoration." Her parents had been assured that, if Una maintained a proper diet and exercised regularly, "we need have no apprehension of future mental disturbance." Once again, Una was kept home from school; the best one in Concord was coeducational, and only Julian was allowed to go. After her recovery, Una enrolled in a nearby girls' gymnastics academy to learn calisthenics.

Down the road in Concord, the Emerson daughters, Edith and Ellen, three and five years older than Una, were being groomed for lives of service to their parents, the often invalided Lidian and the eminent sage Ralph Waldo, known to all as Waldo. Edith resisted the plan, marrying at twenty-four into a wealthy China trade family, making a different sort of contribution to the family's well-being. Ellen, named for her father's first wife, Ellen Tucker Emerson, who'd died of tuberculosis after a year of marriage, remained single. At fourteen she had been sent to a boarding school in the Berkshires, only to be called back a year later, when her father left on an extended lecture tour, to "stay at home and keep house" for her mother. Another year at a girls' academy in Cambridge followed. Then, at seventeen, Ellen embarked on "my career as superintendent of the house," which stretched through the three remaining decades of her parents' lives and beyond, as she helped edit her father's posthumous works.

The Hawthornes' household was not as social as the Emersons', nor did Una's reclusive father travel frequently. She was not pressed into service at an early age. Such a mission might have supplied the "purpose in life" that had eluded her since childhood, but in the end there was no need. Nathaniel fell ill, probably with stomach cancer, and died at sixty the year Una turned twenty. Seven years later, after the surviving family members had moved back to Europe in hopes of eking out a more comfortable living on Nathaniel's royalties, Sophia died of pneumonia in London at sixty-three. Julian had married; Rose was engaged. Exhausted from tending her mother through her final illness and more alone than she'd ever been, Una fell apart. Her aunt Elizabeth Peabody, now a contributor to *The Una* as her reform interests expanded from transcendentalism to woman's rights, crossed the Atlantic to see to her niece's care and reported on the relapse of "violent symptoms" by letter to a trusted family friend.

Elizabeth Peabody, too, might not have written in such detail if she hadn't shared her late brother-in-law's belief that Una's illness was an "entirely physical disease—and amenable to medical treatment." She named her niece's condition "insanity" and "an old story *with us*"—Una's family. After Sophia's death in February 1871, Una had been "insane all summer by fits," during which, Elizabeth wrote, "she always believes, when in them, that some man is in love with her whom it is her duty to marry, or he will die of grief—and she has had this illusion at different times with respect to *eight* different persons!" Elizabeth reached London in the fall after a telegram alerted her that Una's stay at a water cure establishment had ended badly. There, "the mania rose to its height" and "she became dangerous to the life of the servant who had her in charge—by her usual symptom of seizing her and squeezing her from which seizure it took strong men to separate her." Una was sent directly to "the Insane Hospital," where doctors ordered the family never to speak to Una of the delusions she experienced during her fits of derangement: "the most important thing for her [is] that she should not mingle her insane impressions with the sane ones—or she would become *incurable*." Una was twenty-seven years old.

Elizabeth remained in London through the several months of Una's hospitalization, while also helping to settle Sophia's estate, a task that had overwhelmed the Hawthorne children. Una emerged, calm again and intent on taking up charitable work supported by a newly established order of Anglo-Catholic nuns, the Clewer Sisters. She'd joined the Church of England before her mother's death, favoring the congregation at St. Barnabas near the family's home in South Kensington, the first church in England built by Ritualists. Members of a rising faction in the Anglican Church who advocated a return to long-abandoned Catholic practices, the Ritualists conducted services in Latin, opened pews to all free of charge, and founded celibate sisterhoods to serve the poor. Una might even become a Clewer Sister herself.

Traveling on to Rome for a stay with friends before returning to Boston, Elizabeth confided more, and her story found its way into the private diary of the expatriate newspaper columnist Anne Hampton Brewster in a passage recently discovered by the literary historian Etta Madden. Una's insanity had taken a religious turn: "so far had her aberration gone that she imagined she was the Bride of Christ." One morning she'd "wandered off in a half clad condition without shoes only in stockings . . . searching for her Lord—for her dear Spiritual Bride-groom—who would give her peace!" A young woman took pity on the "ill & fainting" Una and brought her home—to a house of prostitution, where at first "Una lay in a torpid senseless state almost as if dead." Then "to the surprise of every one she opened her eyes" and "solemnly began a sort of sermon," which "set all the young strumpets to weeping." After spending a night "under the polluted roof," Una led "the whole covey of feminine reprobates" to St. Barnabas for the morning service, where friends saw her "enter with her strange companions" and afterward entreat the clergyman to "remonstrate and pray with the girls." The friends took Una home.

"What a sad, sad story!" Anne Brewster exclaimed in her diary. And how like the Una of Spenser's poem to have wandered in a "desert of danger," to enter the house of "sin and shame" and emerge "untouched, spotless, and unharmed." Brewster then took up the refrain that would echo through most later writing about Una: she could not be separated from her father's fictions. The whole episode, Brewster wrote, was like something out of Nathaniel Hawthorne's "peculiar romances." And with a father "so impractical, moody[,] filled with all manner of unhealthy imaginings, occupied in every mode of morbid analytical examination of human emotions," Brewster concluded, "no wonder one of the children went mad."

PERHAPS IT WAS because I'd peered into a coffin once myself that I began to entertain questions from a second minor character in my book, the young Ellen Tucker Emerson—Waldo's first wife, for whom he'd named his first daughter, born of his second marriage. How pretty the fair-haired Ellen Tucker had been, although her cheeks were flushed red with illness rather than health—and how talented! Several of the poems she'd written at eighteen, the year she married, made their way into the transcendentalists' literary journal, *The Dial,* alongside poetry by her husband and his friends Thoreau and Fuller a full decade after Ellen's death at age nineteen in 1831.

Waldo mourned Ellen so deeply, found her early death so hard to accept, that over a year afterward, on one of his daily visits to her grave, he opened the tomb and looked inside her coffin. He wanted to "see for himself" what death had done, his biographer Robert Richardson writes. Waldo recorded nothing more than the act, nothing of what he saw. Yet the experience marked him. Five years later, in his first great prose work *Nature,* he wrote, "Even the corpse hath its own beauty."

Ellen wasn't buried in the Emerson family plot. There was no cemetery at Sleepy Hollow in the 1830s, only untamed country-side surrounding a wooded glen. Nor had the newlywed Emersons lived in Concord. I wanted to know where Waldo had visited Ellen, perhaps visit myself—and I found that I could not find out.

Powerfully contagious to those living in close quarters, tuberculosis swept through the Tucker family, as it did the Emersons. Waldo lost a brother and sister in childhood before meeting Ellen, and he would lose another two brothers to the disease during the decade after her death. As a young man, Waldo himself suffered from tuberculosis, which for a painful nine months affected his eyes before sparing him to live into his eighties. Ellen Tucker's father died at forty-nine when she was only nine; he was entombed on the grounds of the family home in Roxbury, then a suburb of Boston. Ellen's older sister, Mary, joined him several years later, as did Ellen herself, soon to be followed by another sister, Margaret, and their mother. When the estate was sold, the Tucker family's remains were moved first to a cemetery in Roxbury and finally to a family plot purchased by Ellen's sole surviving relation, Paulina Tucker Nash, at lavish Mount Auburn Cemetery in Cambridge. This third interment took place in 1878. By the end of the century, the family's Roxbury home was torn down and replaced with a commercial block—brick storefronts all in a row. There was no longer a tomb, not even a parcel of land to visit as Waldo had.

Waldo Emerson was still living in 1878—he was seventy-five. Did the man who had once visited his beloved's grave daily, imploring, "Dost thou not hear me Ellen?" have a say in the place of her ultimate burial? What would Ellen have wanted? In middle age, Waldo had purchased his own family plot in the new cemetery at Sleepy Hollow and moved the remains of his mother, dead in 1853 at eighty-five, and firstborn child, Ralph Waldo Jr., who'd died at five of scarlet fever, to the commanding hillside that would become known as Authors Ridge. Waldo had his mother's remains transferred undisturbed, but on Little Waldo's reinterment again he looked into a coffin and again left no comment.

Nor is there any sign in his surviving letters and journals of 1878 that Waldo had been consulted on Ellen's interment at Mount Auburn. He'd stayed in touch with Paulina, sending her copies of each of his books published since the 1850s. In 1875, he sent *Parnassus*, a five-hundred-page anthology of favorite poetry meant to be read aloud by families at fireside. But for a selection of his own poems that appeared a year later, *Parnassus* was the last work published in his lifetime. Along with well-known verses by Chaucer, Milton, and Wordsworth, *Parnassus* included dozens written by Waldo's American contemporaries, most of them friends: Thoreau, Ellery Channing, Ellen Sturgis Hooper. There were none by Ellen Emerson, but Waldo printed his tubercular brother Edward's "The Last Farewell," the twenty-six-year-old's parting thoughts as he sailed out of Boston Harbor to Puerto Rico on what he rightly suspected would be a failed voyage to recover his health. In each stanza Edward bids a fond farewell—to church spire, hometown, mother, brothers—and concludes with the plaintive refrain "Far away, far away." Waldo said his last goodbye to Edward the same year Ellen died.

No, it would not have been fitting, so many decades later, to separate Ellen from her family—if that were even possible. The Concord sage, who had twice seen the work of death and whose own death beckoned five years in the future, knew that much.

I located her ultimate resting place in a secluded dell at Mount Auburn Cemetery, where I brushed aside the ivy that clung to the worn, flat ledger stone listing the names of father, mother, and two sisters and read the bold inscription: "ELLEN TUCKER wife of RALPH WALDO EMERSON." I could not conjure her presence in this rolling green landscape on the outskirts of a city where she had never lived, but I felt the separation of space and time neither Waldo nor Ellen had wanted to endure. "There is one birth & one baptism & one first love and the affections cannot keep their youth any more than men," Waldo had written in his journal five days after Ellen's death, urging himself on to a new life without her. I envisioned, far away in Concord on Authors Ridge, Waldo's own monument—an immense block of iridescent rose quartz rising uncarved and craggy, emblem of the many years he survived Ellen and then his neighbors, Thoreau and Hawthorne, amassing a body of work that still lives. Could he have done all that with Ellen, or had her death somehow enabled his ascent, as if they'd once balanced on a seesaw of fate?

———

I'D VISITED SOPHIA'S AND UNA'S original graves at London's Kensal Green Cemetery in 1989 on a research fellowship. It was only my second trip to Europe, and I'd never seen a hawthorn in bloom before, let alone the lush pink-and-white hedgerows that marked walking paths and the borders of farmlands out my window as I rode the train from Liverpool to London in late May. Kensal Green was a vast expanse of headstones and monuments, and it was a hot afternoon when I arrived, but I looked for the hawthorn tree I knew Una had planted beside Sophia's grave in 1871, and there it was—a great cascading waterfall of pink blossoms sheltering both Hawthorne women and offering me welcome shade. I was far from home, and so were they. But that seemed fitting. It had been their choice to leave America and settle in London, and that's where I found them. Studying the short span of years recorded on Una's stone, I wondered whether Una's death, explained so melodramatically by her brother and thereafter attributed to "a broken heart" by family and friends, had been a suicide.

When I heard about the planned reinterment of Una and Sophia at Sleepy Hollow—the "reunion"—I was troubled by the erasure of the history I'd traced. But nearly two decades had passed since my London pilgrimage, and Sister Mary Joseph told me the hawthorn tree had died and fallen across the headstones, breaking Sophia's in two. The cost to repair and refurbish the site would be significant for the Rosary Hill Home, which had long paid for its maintenance; the decision was made to repatriate the remains of the founder's mother and sister instead. As with the several interments of Ellen Emerson, this was history too. And, by sheer coincidence, the transfer revived my early question concerning suicide, giving me cause to pursue it.

To this day, surviving family members often choose to cover up a suicide, to print the standard euphemism "died unexpectedly" in obituaries. But in mid-nineteenth-century England, there were powerful legal incentives to suppress a "self-murder," then a crime against the Crown, still classified as homicide at the time of Una's death. A person who attempted suicide but failed could receive a lengthy prison term, finally reduced to two years in 1879. Just five years before Una's death in 1877, a corollary law requiring that a suicide's property be turned over to the Crown was rescinded. For centuries, British law mandated the burial of a suicide at a public crossroads with a stake through the heart, to be trampled upon and forgotten. That changed with an 1823 statute, which nevertheless denied a suicide Christian burial rites and required interment after dark—a law still in effect when Una died. A hastily convened court proceeding could remove these penalties by judging the deceased insane, yet, as the historian Barbara Gates writes in *Victorian Suicide*, while the English "openly mourned death and sensationalized murder . . . they seem to have deeply feared suicide and to have concealed it whenever possible."

Charlotte Sterky, proprietress of St. Andrews Cottage, the "Home of rest for Ladies" where Una died, who signed the death certificate as witness, would have had reason to cooperate in concealing a "self-murder" that took place on church grounds. (In the years after Una's death, St. Andrews Cottage required its residents to provide a doctor's attestation of sound mental health.) Una's death certificate lists "pyrosis"—digestive complaints—and "exhaustion" as causes of death. The brief obituary of "Miss Una Hawthorne, a daughter of the American novelist," that appeared in the *South London Chronicle* five days later must have relied on Julian's testimony: after her fiancé died, "she had slowly lost strength, and gradually faded out of life without any specific disease." Julian had known his sister's death would attract press attention, like that of eighteen-year-old Malcolm Melville, son of their father's friend Herman Melville, whose suicide by revolver ten years before was reported in newspapers around the globe. The *Chronicle* added a detail I had not read anywhere else: September was the month in which Una was to have married.

Una could have traveled to Clewer with a lethal dose of laudanum tucked into her traveling bag or a packet of arsenic powder, which her mother had taken in homeopathic "dilutions" as a cure for her frequent headaches. An elixir of arsenic had killed the teenaged poet Thomas Chatterton, whose death by suicide was immortalized in a painting of the 1850s by the Pre-Raphaelite Henry Wallis, picturing a handsome youth stretched full-length on a narrow bed, his pallid face contrasting sharply with copper-red hair, papers strewn about and vial of poison rolling away from a limp hand that grazes the bare wooden floor. Laudanum—morphine powder dissolved in alcohol—was the choice of thirty-two-year-old Lizzie Siddal, muse to the inner circle of the Pre-Raphaelite Brotherhood and a talented painter herself, whose afterlife secured her fame.

It was Siddal whose brilliant red locks and pale complexion established the Pre-Raphaelites' signature motif, after one of their members spotted her at work in a milliner's shop and invited her to pose. Of the many portraits that followed—by Walter Deverell, who discovered Siddal; William Holman Hunt; and Dante Gabriel Rossetti—the best known is John Everett Millais's *Ophelia,* for which Siddal posed long hours in a sopping wet gown, immersed in a bath of water that quickly turned cold. The resulting pneumonia led to her dependence on laudanum. Rossetti painted her most often and made thousands of sketches. The two were lovers; eventually they married. It was Rossetti who found her dead, laudanum bottle drained, suicide note at her side—a note that had to be burned to secure the judgment of insanity required for a Christian burial. The grieving Rossetti placed a manuscript of his poems in her coffin, only to wish them back seven years later. That's when friends entered the cemetery after dark to dig up Lizzie Siddal's coffin and retrieve the poems. Afterward they told Rossetti his wife's pale face was as beautiful as ever, and her hair had grown to fill the coffin, glowing red in the light of the bonfire they'd set to illuminate the excavation: lies meant to console that took hold in the popular imagination.

I returned to Concord to look more closely at Una's portrait, hanging in a stairwell I'd used many times to reach the library's basement archive for research. I'd remembered the red hair, but not the ghostly pallor or the vacant look in the sitter's eyes. I thought of the description of Una at age twenty by the writer-editor Thomas Wentworth Higginson, a family friend who visited the Wayside after Nathaniel's death: "Her magnificent hair blazed and glittered upon me in the doorway most unexpectedly." In Higginson's recollection, Una was "tall beyond the average height of women, absolutely erect. . . . It was this nobleness of carriage which first arrested attention, and her superb Titianesque coloring which afterwards held it—the abundant hair of reddish auburn and the large gray eyes." Walter Deverell had described Lizzie Siddall to his friends in remarkably similar terms: "She's like a queen, magnificently tall, with a lovely figure. . . . [S]he has grey eyes, and her hair is like dazzling copper."

Not surprisingly, the two artists to whom Una's portrait is credited, Henriette Corkran and William Gorman Wills, were exponents of the Pre-Raphaelite school. Corkran had visited Rossetti in his studio and admired his portraits of Siddal. Wills was better known as a playwright, but he, too, painted an ashen, red-haired Ophelia. Corkran's parents maintained a literary salon in South Kensington where Wills often stayed while writing his plays. I knew from Elizabeth Peabody's letter that while she was alive, Sophia Hawthorne discouraged Una from forming a friendship with their neighbors, the "Bohemian" Corkrans. But Una was drawn to their circle in the months after her mother's death, while recovering from her breakdown. "I longed to put on canvas a record of her strange weird personality," the "far-away look in her magnificent eyes," the "glorious amber hair," and the "throat and neck like white Carrara marble," Corkran recalled in a late memoir she titled *Celebrities and I*. Una was "a living modern Ophelia." She was also, Corkran couldn't help adding, "the living embodiment of her illustrious father's heroines—her short history, so pathetic and tragic, would have suited his romantic, weird genius."

Both Higginson and Corkran wrote about Una because she was her father's daughter. Higginson had gone to Concord with the aim of examining Nathaniel's manuscripts, and Una obliged, showing him her father's notebooks and leading him on a walk to the Old Manse, where she'd been born. Higginson paused to read the inscription in the window her mother had made on Una's behalf. "I looked at her and thought it might have been another tale for the *Wonder-Book*," Higginson wrote afterward.

Even Una traded on her father's name. She did not join the Clewer Sisters, as some had expected, nor did she take up "the reform of erring women," as gossip had it back in Concord. But she helped to establish a home for orphans in London, and she solicited financial assistance for the asylum by publishing notices in the *Times:* "Will not some of those who have read my father's works come to our aid?" Her plea in verse, "Hawthorne at Christmas," appeared in *Punch* in December 1872:

> *All ye who've sat tranced in reading*
> HAWTHORNE'S *House of the Seven Gables,*
> *For a Hawthorne-House I'm pleading,*
> *Peopled with fair facts, not fables.*

The poem continues for several stanzas and concludes with the assurance that the funds she sought—three hundred pounds to keep "our little refuge" from closing—will "make HAWTHORNE'S daughter glad."

What could make Hawthorne's daughter glad? Had Una ever been glad? "It was impossible she would ever be happy," a friend who knew her well wrote after Una's death. But was this a grieving friend's retrospective judgment, an effort to lessen the tragedy?

I tried to distinguish fact from fable in the several posthumous accounts of Una's last years I could find, all of them attempts to explain what might in the end have been inexplicable: she had been engaged once before and broken it off—or was jilted; she had been in love with Rose's husband before her little sister married him—or was not; she had known Webster was too sick to live—or she did not. There seemed no end to the back and forth, and some of these rumors, I learned, had made it into newspapers, no doubt exacerbating whatever distress she may actually have felt.

Una had taken Higginson to Sleepy Hollow on his visit to Concord, plucked a bouquet from the periwinkles growing around her father's headstone, and handed it to him. I decided to follow them there. I drove the short distance from the library, past the village green, down Bedford Street and through the cemetery gates to park at the base of Authors Ridge, then climbed a steep, narrow path to the Hawthorne plot on what Higginson had called "a lovely wooded knoll." The oaks and evergreens were taller now and kept the spot in perpetual shade. Nothing but moss was growing on hard earth compacted by the footsteps of literary pilgrims who'd deposited flowers, pencils, and coins at the base of Nathaniel's headstone, despite the low iron chain suspended from granite fence posts meant to keep tourists out. Sophia's and Una's stones, grand Gothic arches of white marble transported from Kensal Green, had been cut down to fit the smaller scale of a New England town cemetery. Still, they dwarfed Nathaniel's simple marker bearing only his last name.

Una's date of death had been excised in the transition, and in the absence of that finality it was tempting—if I'd wanted to follow other writers' leads—to imagine that Una's ambiguous fate had been predicted long ago by her father. "But where was little Pearl?" he'd asked at the end of *The Scarlet Letter*. She'd inherited Roger Chillingworth's fortune and sailed away to some "unknown region." Beyond that, all was conjecture: "If still alive, she must now have been in the flush and bloom of early womanhood. None knew—nor ever learned, with the fulness of perfect certainty—whether the elf-child had gone thus untimely to a maiden grave; or whether her wild, rich nature had been softened and subdued, and made capable of a woman's gentle happiness."

But I would not assist in turning Una Hawthorne into a fiction. That was the lesson of looking inside the coffin. There are a few things we can know for sure: a patch of cloth, a fragment of bone, a red braid. And then there are the questions we can't answer.

The Second Man in the Front Row

*I*T'S AN ICONIC PHOTO, EASILY found on websites devoted to World War I, first sent out to newspapers in 1917, with the caption: "Funeral of the first American soldier killed in battle in France." In a cemetery in the small village of Bathelémont, a French chaplain reads the funeral service as a dozen soldiers stand in formation, eyes trained on the casket poised above the grave, a mound of fresh earth beside it. The sky is gray; a barren wood lines the horizon. One could mark the start of what's come to be called the "American Century" here—it is possible to look back and trace a line from that moment straight to the United States' dominance in world politics at midcentury and beyond.

I look at the photo and see something else: my grandfather Joe Marshall, standing on the right, the second man in the front row, as he put it in a letter home to his parents. Joe is wearing a doughboy helmet and, he points out in the letter, "what looks to be a fur collar." Only the back of his head is visible, and the collar, he explains, is actually the khaki sweater my grandmother, Elizabeth Metcalf Marshall, his bride of six months, knitted for his twenty-eighth birthday, just a few weeks before. My grandfather had not planned to be in the photograph; his face is turned toward the burial, away from the camera. But, as the deputy press officer in charge of photography and film for the American Expeditionary Forces, he'd set up the shot and, later, from his office in Paris, posted the image around the globe.

I knew none of this until, as the centennial of the armistice that ended World War I approached, I decided to look through several boxes of family letters and photographs to learn what I could of my grandparents' war experience. My grandfather was a retired life insurance salesman in his seventies when I knew him best—if I knew him at all. He was tall and thin; in memory, a blur of gray hair, gray wool cardigans and trousers. When I was growing up in Southern California in the 1960s, my family of five would join my grandparents, who lived one town over, for dinners on Sundays and holidays. My grandfather maintained a nearly mute formality, speaking more words in French, sotto voce, with my grandmother, than in English. My grandparents had lived in Paris through the war. Their first child, my uncle Joe Jr., had been born there. That much I knew.

There were hints of an adventurous life before the war. The small mahogany yo-yo, for instance, which my older brother, younger sister, and I took turns playing with after dinner, and which my father said was the first yo-yo to reach America, was brought back by my grandfather from the Philippines, in 1915. My father told me, too, about a poem that his father recited to his children every night at bedtime. "Day by day I float my paper boats one by one down the running stream," it went. "In big black letters I write my name on them and the name of the village where I live. / I hope that someone in some strange land will find them and know who I am." It was written by the Bengali poet Rabindranath Tagore, who received the Nobel Prize in Literature in 1913. My grandfather had met him, my father said, at Tagore's ashram, outside Calcutta (now Kolkata).

These few facts didn't square with the silent elderly gentleman at the head of the dinner table, forgotten by everyone but my grandmother, a children's librarian, who coaxed his appetite with real butter for his white bread and mint jelly for his slice of lamb. And, in some ways, the letters I read, half a century later, only deepened the mystery. But they also brought to life the man in the photograph and reminded me how much we lose when we turn away from the past.

———————

THE FUNERAL THAT my grandfather witnessed at the front was not, in fact, the first American burial in the war. It was the ninth. There had been no members of the press on hand for the first one. It was not Joe's first glimpse of the war: he had lived in wartime Paris for six months two years before, mastering French in preparation, he hoped, for a diplomatic career. In those months he'd come to recognize "the look of the trenches" in the eyes of soldiers returning from the front, many of them grievously maimed, and he knew of the protracted, deadly stalemates that characterized most of the war's battles, months-long contests that moved the front lines a few kilometers at the cost of hundreds of thousands of lives.

But that day in Bathelémont was Joe's first sight of the war up close. He and the journalists whom he ferried by limousine from Paris had come to photograph American soldiers in the trenches and to interview survivors of the first German raid to result in the deaths of American enlisted men. Dropped off outside the village, Joe and his press corps trailed an American Expeditionary Forces sergeant across a muddy field that ran between the two lines of fire; enemy shells landed on the crest of the hill toward which they were climbing, then, mercifully, as the men approached, shifted to targets behind them, "plunking down in the field from which we had come" and making "a nasty noise," as he wrote in a letter home. "You hear the report of the cannon; then a ripping tearing sound, sometimes a thud, then the explosion." At each "crack" of a German battery, he explained, with impressive understatement, "there is a moment of very real interest as you listen for the whine of the shell" to discover its direction.

Joe and his crew reached safety in "a perfect labyrinth" of trenches and were given canes to keep from slipping on the round sticks that served as flooring in the mud. An officer guided them to the "calm sector," where the first American troops to reach the front had been moved into position in late October, and where the German raid had taken place under cover of darkness. The enemy encampment was a mere five hundred yards away, across no-man's-land. Joe peered cautiously over the edge of the trench, glimpsing a tangle of barbed wire at the bottom of a steep incline and the ridge of German trenches beyond. He imagined the confusion and terror that must have gripped the Americans, still unfamiliar with the layout of the trenches and expecting at least a modicum of calm. A medical officer told of finding one of the dead, Thomas Enright, "with his throat cut and every evidence of having put up a desperate struggle." Shreds of German uniform were strewn about, and the ground was scuffed up. The doctor had pocketed the lethal weapon, "straight-bladed" like a paring knife, and showed Joe its wooden handle with two indentations—notches, the doctor supposed, registering the number of men killed with it.

But Joe had come to "make some pictures." The shadowy trenches proved troublesome to photograph, and word of an American burial in progress suggested a better opportunity. Four American soldiers bore the coffin, followed by a French honor guard, then American and French officers, and, last, an American firing squad. A bugler blew taps, the squad fired three volleys, and the coffin was lowered in what was, Joe wrote to his parents, "a touching ceremony for all of us." He walked to the end of the cemetery, where the first three American graves were now protected by low wooden fences. As he copied down the names— Enright, Hay, Gresham—he rested his notebook on the railing and found it difficult to keep from flinching as the nearby batteries continued to crack. Six more graves had been dug in line with the first three, and Joe saw "names from many different ethnic backgrounds, all young Americans caught in the war."

JOE'S INTEREST IN world affairs had been sparked four years earlier, when, as a college senior at Harvard, he'd heard Tagore lecture on Indian philosophy. A transfer student from the University of Kansas, Joe spent more hours at his fraternity and with the glee club than on his studies—until Tagore's message, of "the harmony that exists between the individual and the universal," took hold of him. The Marshall family was moneyed, having parlayed the financial success of a general store in the early days of Kansas settlement into extensive holdings in cornfields, and Joe embarked on a world tour after graduation, stopping for as long as he was welcome in the homes of new friends whom he met sailing first-class from San Francisco to Hawaii, Japan, the Philippines, and, finally, India.

Reaching Calcutta at the end of July 1914, he looked up his former Harvard classmates Jatindra Nath Set and Hira Lal Roy—partisans, he soon learned, in the fledgling Indian independence movement that Tagore was helping to lead. They offered to take him to meet Gurudeb, as the poet was now known to his followers, at his nearby ashram, Santiniketan, "the abode of peace." When Joe arrived at the collection of low white buildings set around a spreading banyan tree on a broad and vacant plain, he was ushered into Tagore's presence by the poet's son-in-law, who must have startled Joe with his declaration that "out of the millions of people in America you are the one who has been selected to come and visit us, to bring us their message, and take ours in return. . . . East and West have now met here at Santiniketan and you must not leave until we have time to understand each other." Over a breakfast of tea, toast, and mangoes with a berobed Tagore, Joe promised to return for a longer stay. The conversation had "a soothing effect," Joe reported, despite the guru's dire prediction: "Europe is as the setting sun. It has risen in its greatness and power by unnatural means; and as the sun sinks in a flood of red light, so Europe will sink in a flood of red blood."

Had Tagore received the news without telling Joe? Or were powers of divination at work? When Joe got back to Calcutta, he learned that Austria-Hungary had declared war on Serbia and that Germany had declared war on Russia and France. On the day that Joe was meant to return to the ashram, Great Britain declared war on Germany.

Remarkably, Joe did not immediately curtail his world travels. But, stalled in Darjeeling with a case of malaria, his previously vague ambitions began to coalesce: to marry and to do something to help France and its allies. He would spend a semester in Paris perfecting his French, and he would intensify his correspondence with Elizabeth Metcalf, the slight, rosy-cheeked Wellesley girl from Detroit, whom he'd met in the parlor of his fraternity after a Harvard-Yale game and who was called "Sunbeam" by her friends on the sailing and tennis teams. When he returned to America, in late 1915, he organized a series of concerts in ten Kansas cities— he'd sing "Invictus"—and raised ten thousand dollars for the Kansas Belgian Relief Fund he had established. And he proposed to Elizabeth. They celebrated their engagement with a gala party in April 1917, the same month that Congress voted to declare war on Germany.

The couple had planned to settle in Kansas City, but Joe, instead, traveled to Washington, D.C., to work his connections with government men he'd met on his world tour. At the end of May, he telegraphed Elizabeth. His language skills had merited him a commission as a special interpreter to General John J. Pershing; he would soon leave for France. "I love you with all my heart," he wrote. He was boarding a train to Detroit that night. "Will you marry me Thursday evening?"

On the day of their wedding, Joe learned that he would not be allowed to travel on Pershing's military transport—there were too many interpreters on board. Joe and Elizabeth enjoyed a brief honeymoon in Washington, still believing they would be separated, until Joe gained permission to sail on a French passenger ship as a civilian. He could bring Elizabeth.

After crossing the Atlantic on *La Touraine*, a vessel carrying the volunteer ambulance corps of several East Coast colleges, the two settled in a pension on rue Vaneau, convenient to both AEF headquarters and the Alliance Française. Elizabeth, who'd spent the previous year teaching in a girls' school to help with her family's finances, began studying French literature and art. At a time when other American couples who married hastily in the shadow of war were separated by a vast and dangerously mined ocean, Elizabeth could join Joe after work for performances at the Opéra-Comique. They could pack their treasured French picnic basket for a Sunday outing at Versailles—where, Elizabeth wrote in her diary, "we didn't try to go everywhere, secure in the thought that we would go many times."

JOE'S RISE FROM interpreter to press officer, with the rank of second lieutenant, was rapid. He had toyed with photography at Harvard and on his world travels, and somehow he managed to pick up film-editing skills as well; these were still new technologies that many of his elders could scarcely fathom. By the time Joe went to the front, in November 1917, he was supervising six hundred men: "operators, developers, censors, stenographers, messengers, etc." It was a job that "requires *vision*," he wrote home, "for there are no precedents to guide me." He would leave the army as Captain Marshall.

Joe often credited life with Elizabeth for his success. He pitied his fellow officers, who would "wander aimlessly about the hotel lobbies smoking innumerable cigarettes, plainly bored and lonesome." How much better it was to come home for a convivial meal at the pension with his wife and the other boarders, then retire to their fifth-floor room, pull their "big aristocratic armchair" up to the French windows, open them wide, and curl up together, gazing at the sunset and the Eiffel Tower. "In the midst of excitement and stress and sorrow, we two are keeping our heads and living simple normal lives," Joe wrote.

The Marshall family's cornfields had been suffering disastrous growing seasons, with too much and then too little rain, and the couple mostly lived on Joe's lieutenant's salary, the first he'd ever earned. Elizabeth, already accustomed to economizing, didn't mind. "We are just ridiculously in love," she confided to her mother, and "we never could have stood it apart from each other." As for the narrow bed the pension provided, she wrote, "Here's a real Marshall secret—we *prefer* it narrow."

Without realizing it, Elizabeth had conceived during their May honeymoon, or perhaps on the Atlantic crossing. In August, an American doctor explained her summerlong queasiness by confirming the pregnancy. She continued attending classes at the Alliance Française, which permitted her to tour museums and cathedrals closed to the public in wartime. Her mother was a tireless clubwoman who kept insisting that Elizabeth "do something" for the war effort, but, with a baby on the way, Elizabeth felt she was doing plenty. She read the Paris papers daily and summarized the news for Joe; occasionally she aided him in translation work. "I haven't forgotten that I can be of use," she assured her mother, but "homes and babies and knowledge—those things have to go on well, too." In the weeks before the baby's due date, Germany launched a campaign of aerial attacks on Paris with its heavy Gotha bombers. Joe took out an expensive "war risk" life insurance policy; when, on January 30, a bomb was dropped straight through the house across from theirs and then merely "thumped out into the street," going off like a "fizzer" instead of exploding, the couple joked about Joe's prescience in saving a monthly premium by setting the policy to start on February 1. That same night, a bomb landed on the Crédit Lyonnais where Joe received occasional cable transfers from his father. It blew out the corner of the building, killing two.

Two weeks later, on Valentine's Day, Elizabeth was playing four-hand piano duets with her landlady when labor commenced. At the American hospital in Neuilly-sur-Seine, a suburb of Paris, Joe was allowed to attend the birth, talking his Sunbeam through what proved to be an easy labor. (The doctor credited Elizabeth's "athletic life and ability to relax.") Elizabeth savored a compulsory monthlong recuperation at the hospital, but when she and the baby returned to the pension, she couldn't sleep, and her breast milk stopped flowing—small wonder when blasts from "la grosse Bertha," a German cannon, interrupted a nighttime feeding, or a fire engine, that "machine of noise and horror," raced down rue Vaneau, warning of an air strike, "leaving in its place only a nameless questioning of the sky above us." Joe Jr. was losing weight.

In May, Joe and Elizabeth traveled to Île-aux-Moines, a coastal island in Brittany, where there was a small American colony, fresh sea air, and a milk cow for the baby. Joe could only spend the night, but, after one week in a hotel, Elizabeth made up her mind to rent a house and stay for the summer. ("I believe it's the first time in my life that I ever decided anything for myself," she wrote to Joe, on May 24, their first anniversary.) Their families back in Kansas and Michigan begged Joe to send Elizabeth and the baby home, but Joe refused, stressing the value of living through "these tremendous events *together*." He doubted if "a thousand years at Detroit or Kansas City could ever have brought us to the same degree of mutual respect and love and understanding that this year in Paris has given us." And "we haven't let anything make us sad either," he claimed. "There is so much sorrow now that it is one's duty to be gay and happy just to show others that the world hasn't gone all to pieces after all."

Still, a note of desperation crept into his defense. "We are in this cursed business to do our full duty," he wrote. Censorship rules prevented him from explaining his work and the "influence it may have on the war" to his parents, "but Elizabeth *knows*," he went on. Elizabeth knew, too, that Joe wasn't well—he'd also been losing weight. In late June, he checked into a Red Cross hospital in Paris with the Spanish flu. The attending surgeon prescribed a three-week leave, writing in his orders that Captain Marshall "is much debilitated from over-work." He would spend the time in Brittany.

Joe arrived at Île-aux-Moines believing the war might go on for another two years. As he rested in the shade of a fig tree in the garden behind the seaside cottage that Elizabeth had rented, his infant son napping in a carriage beside him, he considered how all five of his commanding officers had stepped down from exhaustion, nervous breakdowns, or illness, often leaving him in charge. It was not "an easy sort of work." Three junior officers had been required to fill his place while on leave.

Then, while Joe was still in Brittany, a major military counteroffensive from the Allies brought the grinding Second Battle

of the Marne to a close. The Germans were finally outmaneu-
vered by a swarm of Allied tanks at Reims, the cathedral town
ninety miles from Paris. When Joe returned to work in August,
the mood in the press office had shifted. Paris was safer now. "No
one can overestimate the part the Americans played in turning
the tide," Joe wrote home. In September, Elizabeth and the baby
returned from Île-aux-Moines to a "cute little house" Joe had
rented in Le Vésinet, "the most modern" of the Parisian suburbs.
Joe had regained his energy, if not his weight. "Every hour, these
days, is so filled with the present that there is very little time to
look backward," he wrote home on his twenty-ninth birthday,
October 11.

One month later, Joe jimmied his way through a locked door
at the Chambre des Députés and pressed forward into the packed
assembly hall to hear Georges Clemenceau, "the grand old man
of the war," announce the terms of the armistice. The prime minister read out all thirty-four paragraphs in a clear, matter-of-fact
voice, Joe wrote afterward, "and it made my blood tingle to hear
those words." Each article brought renewed applause until Clemenceau silenced the crowd to issue his own words of gratitude
to the "glorious armies" and "render honor to the brave men
who had given their lives for freedom and justice and humanity."
Then someone started "La Marseillaise," and "the whole assembly took it up with a swing that was great." Joe sang until the
tears rolled down his cheeks.

––––––––––

JOE WAS GRANTED an honorable discharge in January 1919 and
commended as an officer of "attractive personality, well dis-

ciplined, and with executive ability." He might have taken his family home, but he'd rented the house in Le Vésinet until May. "I don't know of any young couple who will start out in the 're-construction' period with better preparation," Joe wrote to his parents, explaining the decision to stay on through the spring. He'd always believed his work in the press office would give him "the most valuable experience for after-life." He and Elizabeth were "anxious to whirl into the adventure." Joe planned to spend the few months writing a book on Clemenceau, and he offered himself to *The Kansas City Star* as a Paris correspondent to report on the peace process. But before the ink on his letter was dry, he'd received an invitation to serve for six months as "publicity man" for the newly formed League of Red Cross Societies, "about the biggest thing that is happening these surprising days," he wrote in a letter home. With a salary three times his army pay, the job was "the greatest opportunity for service that has ever come my way."

It would require two weeks of meetings in July, at Geneva, where the league's permanent headquarters were to be established. Before heading there, Joe took a Sunday off for a final French picnic with Elizabeth, an excursion by train to "the devastated regions" around Reims where the Yanks had proved themselves in battle. The couple packed their basket with sliced veal sandwiches, strawberries, and a thermos of hot chocolate, and joined a crowd with the same outing in mind at the Gare de l'Est. Just past Château-Thierry, Elizabeth wrote, they began to see the results of war: "Dear little villages nestling at the foot of a hill and surrounded by well-kept green fields," and yet with church steeples toppled, walls razed, thatched roofs collapsed. She wondered where the farmers lived who cultivated those

fields. Nearing Reims, they came upon "a vast plain of desola-
tion," riven with trenches, blanketed in red poppies. She plucked
a blossom to enclose in her letter. As for the city of Reims, "it was
so sad and terrible—not a single untouched house . . . nobody,
nothing there," she wrote. Joe and Elizabeth gazed up at the cathedral's massive walls and buttresses and saw sky.

When Joe returned from Geneva, he had a decision to make.
"The choice has come between moving to Geneva for another
year or coming home to you," Elizabeth relayed to their parents.
Joe wrote a few days later of the "real opportunity" to make the
Red Cross "my 'life work' if I were so inclined."

Stay, I wanted to tell my grandparents, as I read their words—
this is the "after-life" you prepared for, not the dreary years spent
peddling life insurance policies to the neighbors in Southern
California. But there was more. "Perhaps we have done wrong in
always writing you such optimistic letters," Joe wrote: "we didn't
want you to worry," he added. Elizabeth supplied the details: Joe
was "tired and thin," perhaps suffering a recurrence of malaria.
"Traveling is difficult, food scarce." Finally: "We want to see you
and be with you and start our life in America."

In August, Joe rallied to join an eight-member Inter-Allied
Medical Mission, in the newly established Polish Republic,
where, Elizabeth wrote, the Red Cross "has been given the tremendous work of handling the typhus epidemic" originating
in eastern Europe. This time Joe took the photographs himself, converting the best of them to glass lantern slides, so that
they could be projected at public lectures or in presentations to
governmental bodies. He secured a set of fourteen slides of his
own—striking scenes of destitute families, refugees in freight
cars, a "sad-eyed Polish peasant" whose wife and children had

died of typhus as refugees in Russia. "Drugs, hospital supplies, and clothing are urgently needed," Joe's captions read. "A very severe epidemic will occur this winter unless the necessary equipment and supplies are received to enable the medical authorities to deal energetically with the situation." Joe carried the packet of slides with him in October 1919, when he and Elizabeth sailed home with Joe Jr., their "Petit Parisien," on the same French liner on which they'd shipped out. In snapshots, their wide smiles suggest that they were eager to return.

———————

THE FIRST YEAR home, however, brought private losses more painful than anything they'd experienced abroad. Joe's mother succumbed to the tuberculosis she'd suffered from for more than a decade. Elizabeth's favorite sister died in childbirth, losing her baby. The young son of a beloved cousin died that year too. My father, Joe and Elizabeth's second child, born in December 1920, was given the little boy's name.

When Joe had received the special interpreter commission, he'd written to his parents, "I will know all the inside history of the greatest of all wars." Did he ever start writing his book on Clemenceau, or another he'd planned about his own wartime experiences? He had made carbon copies of his letters to work from, but I found no outlines or drafts. In 1920, he ran for a seat in the House of Representatives, on the slogan "Send a Soldier to Congress," but he didn't win. Joe had lived through the war from its beginning, in August 1914, until its end, more than four years later. His campaign was out of step with his fellow Kansans, who'd had only a brief experience of the war and may have preferred to forget.

Joe's disappointment over the election may have prompted the family's move west. As the Marshall cornfields in Kansas steadily failed, Joe scraped together enough cash to buy two neighboring house lots in Altadena, California. He planned to build and flip houses, as we'd say today. But, after the first bungalow was finished, California's real estate crash of the 1920s rendered the scheme useless. My grandparents sold the next-door lot at a loss and simply stayed.

When Joe and Elizabeth were first in France, in the summer of 1917, Joe had told his parents in a letter that, through college and his world travels, he'd often "thought I was in a false position outside of the main channel of life and affairs." Then the war had come along, he wrote, "the *realest* piece of business the U.S. ever tackled." Perhaps he felt the insubstantiality of his position once again when he returned to Kansas, bearing fourteen glass slides picturing a destitute people in a feudal landscape, each one numbered and keyed to a caption with information of no consequence to anyone he knew.

But the truth is, I don't know how he felt. I didn't really know my grandfather and, in the way of our impecunious family, did not even fly home for Joe's funeral, when he died while I was away at college in New England—no one had considered the price of my plane ticket a worthy expenditure. By then we'd given a name to what had become more than a habit of silence at the dinner table: senility. At Thanksgiving the year before I left for college, he'd gotten up from the table, unnoticed, and disappeared. My grandmother cruised the neighboring streets in her aged Chevy until she found him pacing the sidewalk, agitated, lost.

What I'd discovered of my grandparents' lives in their letters was so much more impressive, so much more *interesting*, than anything I'd imagined. Why had I not heard any of these stories? Why had I not searched for my grandparents sooner in the brown cardboard boxes that arrived from California in the late 1980s, after they had died? I'd stacked the boxes in an attic closet and left them there while I read the letters of people unrelated to me and wrote up their lives instead.

Perhaps, as the years passed, Joe could manage only so much self-invention to meet a changing world. Disappointment may have grown to eclipse what was once a matter of pride, or even rendered the early accomplishment a shameful point of comparison. Or perhaps the war and what Joe saw of its effects in France and Poland were so horrendous that "accomplishment" didn't signify. "Think of the stories we can tell our grandchildren of our experiences in Paris during the great war of 1917," Joe had written to his parents, defending his decision to bring Elizabeth along with him. But he never did.

FREE FOR A WHILE

*M*Y FIRST YEAR OF SCHOOL was interrupted in early spring 1960 when my family moved from a small ranch house in Los Altos, then a bedroom suburb of San Francisco surrounded by mustard fields and rolling hills dotted with California live oaks, to a two-story Colonial in Pasadena, a city of more than one hundred thousand, about three hundred miles to the south. Despite the larger house, this was no step up. My dad had lost his job as a city planner for Santa Clara County after drinking too much at an office party, a blunder he would repeat to similar effect in future years, and we were retreating to the city of his youth. A childhood friend had found him a job in Los Angeles, a half hour drive down the Pasadena Freeway, the oldest freeway in the country, which started (or ended) at our new hometown.

I was sad to leave my kindergarten friends behind in Los Altos and sensitive to the cloud of shame that trailed us. You can see all that in my face in a photograph taken at the Pasadena

Central Library the summer after our move. My father's mother, nearing retirement in her job as children's librarian, was known for her weekly vacation story hour, and a photographer from a local newspaper had come to document her work. The picture is a snapshot of the multiracial community Pasadena was and still is, though the photo is misleading about the extent of racial mixing in the city, both then and now. The story group had moved outside to the building's hacienda-style courtyard after listening to my grandmother's program of tales gleaned from the folk traditions of five continents, chosen to appeal to an audience of children who could trace their ancestries back, at varying distances, to Africa, Mexico, Japan, China, and Europe. I'm standing in the center of the back row, wearing a striped T-shirt. Also standing, second from the left, is Denise Houlemard, the beaming seven-year-old who would grow up to become one of our high school's first Black homecoming queens during our senior year.

I recognized Denise when I came across the photograph recently and wondered if she'd ever brought Jonathan Jackson, her across-the-street playmate and fellow student at St. Andrew Catholic School, to story hour. I didn't know him then; that would come later, when both Denise and Jonathan shifted into public high school. But I calculated that 1960, the year of the story hour photograph, also marked the last time Jonathan had seen his older brother, George, outside prison or a courtroom. Jailed at eighteen with a sentence of one year to life after accepting a plea deal over a seventy-dollar gas station robbery, George Jackson began reading Marx, Lenin, Trotsky, and Mao, as one year stretched to four and then ten. He joined other "black guerrillas" on the inside working to transform "the black criminal mentality into a black revolutionary mentality," George would write in the introduction to *Soledad Brother,* a collection of his prison letters that rocketed him to fame when it was published in November 1970. A dozen of those letters were written in 1969 to Jonathan, by then my classmate in AP English and U.S. history and a strong student in a tough chemistry class taught by one of our school's few Black teachers, Lee F. Browne.

The summer before our senior year (and Denise's coronation), Jonathan traveled north to visit his brother with a plan to gain his release. On August 7, 1970, Jonathan carried a sack of weapons and a rifle concealed beneath his trench coat into the Marin County courthouse in San Rafael, one of several Frank Lloyd Wright–designed buildings in the futuristic Marin County Civic Center complex. On trial inside was James McClain, a Black San Quentin inmate accused of stabbing a white prison guard. McClain's was one of several cases pending against Black radicals in California state penitentiaries, including that of Jonathan's brother, George, accused, along with two other inmates of Soledad State Prison—the "Soledad Brothers" we heard about on the evening news—of killing a white guard. If convicted, George faced execution by the state.

Pulling a carbine from his bag and shouting, "Okay, this is it! Everyone freeze!" Jonathan took charge of the courtroom, arming McClain and two other San Quentin inmates on hand to testify. The quartet took hostages: the judge, three jurors, and an assistant DA. Jonathan demanded the immediate release of his brother and his Soledad comrades in exchange for the hostages' lives. In the ensuing melee, the judge and two of the San Quentin prisoners were killed; the assistant DA was paralyzed. Seventeen-year-old Jonathan was dead, too, sprayed with bullets in the front seat of the rented van he'd planned to drive to a nearby airport, where he'd meet George and his ardent supporter, Angela Davis, in whose name two of the weapons were registered, and hijack a plane to freedom in Algeria, where the Black Panther leader Eldridge Cleaver was then in exile.

———————

MY UPBRINGING IN Pasadena was the result of my father's disabling mood swings and would always be shadowed by them. I spent my years there looking for a way out, and once I was gone, at seventeen, I rarely returned. My brother, sister, and I were latchkey kids from early grade school, when our mother took the first in a series of low-paying jobs to support the family. My parents wore clothes scavenged from the Clothes Line, a charity shop; I wore cut-rate dresses and shoes from the Sears catalog and J.C. Penney until I learned to sew in seventh grade home economics. My mom clipped coupons from the newspaper on Wednesday nights and drove from market to market chasing bargains on her way home from work, trading in pan drippings, collected in a coffee can that sat on the back of the stove, for a penny a pound at the butcher. One day I found a notice from the gas company taped to our front door, warning that our heat would be turned off for lack of payment; my librarian grandmother took care of the shortfall then and other times, though she had little to spare. When I was seven, she made my older brother, younger sister, and me memorize her phone number in case of trouble at home.

Jonathan's family had moved to Pasadena a few years before mine. Lester Jackson, Jonathan's father, worked for the U.S. Post Office, then one of few available routes to Black middle-class prosperity. Jonathan's mother, Georgia, took care of the household and children, three girls and two boys, all born in Illinois. Before the move west, Lester earned enough to send his older children to Chicago's parochial schools, though his second child, George, balked at the discipline and got into trouble with the police. Lester brought fourteen-year-old George with him to Los Angeles in 1955—the year another Chicago fourteen-year-old, Emmett Till, was brutally murdered in Mississippi—in hopes of giving the boy a fresh start. The rest of the family followed, settling first in Watts and then in a bungalow in Northwest Pasadena, where Lester, with another good job at the post office, again sought a Catholic school education for his children.

A first-generation Chinese American classmate from junior high emailed me over the summer as our fiftieth high school reunions loomed. He was looking up friends from our years at McKinley Junior High, 1965–68, before we matriculated to different high schools. Dennis Wun had gone on to John Muir High School with other students from his mostly Black Northwest Pasadena neighborhood, where the Jacksons lived. My dad had been class president at Muir in 1938, before the Great Migration's second wave made Northwest Pasadena home to the largest Black community in Southern California outside Watts. But I'd gone to Blair, a new high school built on a strip of land next to a power plant at the mouth of the Pasadena Freeway, within walking distance of my house.

Blair High School opened in 1964 with a racial balance mirroring that of the city at large, and if it hadn't been for academic

tracking, a system rife with race prejudice, all the classes would
have looked like my grandmother's story hour group. Instead, as
at McKinley, only PE and required basic courses like civics and
driver's ed were truly mixed. Depending on whom you ask, Blair
was either a project of integrationist zeal or a last-ditch effort to
stave off a busing order that came down anyway in 1970, the end
result of school desegregation suits brought against the city by
Black parents, starting in 1961. Pasadena had a third, virtually
all-white school, Pasadena High School, where Jonathan spent a
few days at the start of his tenth grade year, transferring in from
the parochial school where he'd completed ninth grade. Then
he switched to Blair. Lester Jackson believed his youngest child
and second son should lead a less sheltered life than the Catholic
schools offered, but not at predominantly Black Muir.

I didn't live in a mansion, like the lawyer's son who invited
the junior high chess club over to play on the sets in his oak-
paneled living room. I later quit the club; Dennis, whose father
had emigrated with his wife from mainland China in 1947 as a
"paper son," stayed. But neither he nor Jonathan could have
lived in my Pasadena neighborhood, which, decades before,
when the houses were built, had been covenanted to prevent
non-white families from buying in. The pattern stuck, enforced
by local realtors. The house on the corner, a red gingerbread
Victorian sometimes used in filming Purina Cat Chow commer-
cials, might have been around on November 6, 1885, the date
that came to be known as Black Friday, after Chinese business
owners and their families were driven out of the city center when
a white mob set fire to their rented shop buildings. Pasadena's
first racial zoning ordinance, restricting "Chinese quarters" to
the city's outer limits, was drafted then. On the next street over

from mine was the house later used in filming the *Father of the Bride* remakes, and I could ride my bike to a section of broad lawns leading up to Italianate villas, one of them the Mulwrays' palatial residence in *Chinatown*. Across the street from my own white-clapboard, green-shuttered Colonial was a rare one-story adobe where Albert Einstein lived for a year when he taught at Caltech in the early 1930s. He walked the mile to his office at the institute, whose professors' kids attended McKinley with Dennis and me in the 1960s. A close friend's father, a Caltech wunderkind turned JPL engineer, moved his family east at the end of our ninth grade year for a job he couldn't talk about—he'd been appointed director of the Advanced Research Projects Agency, I later learned, the Defense Department's think tank whose innovations included Arpanet, the precursor of the internet.

While my father withdrew from the world, my mother found solace in civic engagement, after work and in spare weekend hours. She'd given up watercolor painting in favor of woodcuts, and as the crises of the mid-1960s arrived, she made politics her subject. The winter of 1963–64 brought a portrait of the grieving Rose Kennedy; 1965, a scene featuring Sister Mary Antona Ebo among other sober-faced marchers on the road from Selma to Montgomery, led by Martin Luther King Jr. She heard him speak that summer, at Pasadena's Friendship Baptist Church, where he'd last appeared in 1960, telling his audience, "The Negro cannot be free in Pasadena or Los Angeles until the Negro is free in Jackson, Mississippi, and Montgomery, Alabama. We are all involved in a single struggle." By 1965, speaking one month before the Watts Rebellion, King surely knew the adverse conditions his Black listeners faced in California. My mother joined liberal women from our church and the city's activist, integrated YWCA in fighting Proposition 14, a ballot measure that succeeded in overturning the state's 1963 Rumford Fair Housing Act, a law banning racial discrimination by landlords, realtors, and homeowners. I still have one of her campaign buttons—"Would you want your daughter to marry a realtor?"

During my years at McKinley, my mother took a drafting job with the Pasadena Planning Commission. On tight deadline to deliver a series of maps supporting the Pepper Project, a plan for urban renewal centered around Pepper Street in Northwest Pasadena, she brought home rolls of paper and multicolored pencils to work at a drafting table she'd set up in our family room, color-coding city blocks to signify racial composition, while my siblings and I watched TV. She described to us her boss's plan to replace dilapidated housing (rats had been found in basements, she said) with architect-designed town house apartments clustered around a community center with shops and recreational facilities, including a swimming pool. This would be no massive high-rise disaster like the Pruitt-Igoe towers of St. Louis. Did my mother know that one of the houses slated for demolition in the city's urban renewal plan was the childhood home of Muir High graduate Jackie Robinson at 121 Pepper Street? The Robinsons had moved there in 1920 as the first Black family on the block, and Mrs. Robinson still lived at the address. If my mother had been aware that Mrs. Robinson and her neighbors saw nothing substandard about their homes (the rats may have been a fiction put forth by city officials), would she still have believed the Pepper Project was for the good? But how could she, or her boss, not have known? Jackie Robinson was a local hero.

In later years, before her death in 1991, my mother became an ardent preservationist, a member of the Society of Architectural

Historians, whose entry "Public Housing in California" in its online reference, Archipedia, describes the malign forces at work
beyond the reach of the Pasadena Planning Commission's blin-
dered optimism. Foremost was HUD's requirement that, in order
to qualify for federal funding, all new low-income housing units
had to replace existing "slum" units on a one-for-one basis. The
incentive to identify "urban blight" was high. HUD would not
support expansion, only "renewal"—raze a neighborhood and
start again. Then, by the late '60s, when construction was completed on the Pepper Project homes designed by the California
modernists Carl Maston and Ray Kappe and documented by the
renowned photographer Julius Shulman, a new city government
had gained power, forcing out my mother's boss and nixing the
plan's amenities: community center, shopping area, swimming

pool. In the end, the mostly Black residents whose houses had been taken by eminent domain at below-market rates were too well-off to qualify for housing in the Pepper Project, yet couldn't afford to rent or buy in Pasadena. Many displaced Black Pasadenans moved farther north into Altadena, an "unincorporated" region governed by Los Angeles County, though still within the Pasadena Unified School District.

Another famous Black Muir High graduate, the science-fiction writer Octavia Butler, was born in 1947, the year Dennis Wun's parents arrived in the United States. That year, Black Pasadenans succeeded in integrating the city's public swimming pool, the Brookside Plunge. Until 1947, Black families could swim only on Tuesdays, after which the pool was drained and refilled. When I took swimming lessons at Brookside in the early '60s, Butler was already writing fantasy tales as a bookish young teenager; chances are good my grandmother was the storyteller she credited with introducing her to the library. Later, reading Butler's *Parable* novels of the 1990s, I recognized her fictional Southern California city, Robledo, as Pasadena with its long north-south avenue, Los Robles, dividing east from west: a flawed paradise riven by destructive forces, external and internal, from which one was lucky to escape with one's life.

———

WE'RE BORN INTO this world "Not with purpose, / But with potential," Butler's embattled characters recite, lines from "Earthseed," a prayer meant to inspire an empowering fatalism: change is life's only certainty. Fifteen- and sixteen-year-olds are all potential in search of purpose, ever-changing.

Jonathan's class photo from sophomore year, his first at our three-year high school, shows a sleepy-eyed youngster, crisp white collar poking out above a smart crewneck sweater, a hint of the altar boy he'd been at St. Andrew. He looks more twelve than fifteen. A few months later, Jon, as we knew him, was playing JV basketball, making use of his height. His hair was longer, and in the team photo his eyes reveal a sadness that adds poignance to the steady gaze in his junior class photo, taken in the fall of 1969—the year he turned sixteen and got the keys to the family car.

Now he could drive to school, where, due to a city budget shortfall, one class period had been dropped from our daily schedules. School ended at 1:15 p.m. When I think back over the events of 1969–70, the school year that ended with Jonathan's death, I keep coming back to the extra hour we had to ourselves that stretched our sun-drenched afternoons and turned school into a part-time endeavor.

In the early months of junior year, Jon used the car to spend time after school with his friend Michael Dorn, the future TV actor best known for playing Worf in the *Star Trek* franchise. They hung out with two senior girls who lived a few blocks away from me. One of them remembers Mike as the extrovert; Jon was "well-dressed and thoughtful" and carried a thin brown leather briefcase. She recalls his "most beautiful blue-ish eyes" and how he "both watched and listened" with them. Jon was quiet in class too. "He wasn't a speechmaker," his older brother, George, would say, "and neither am I." But both Jackson brothers could write.

We wouldn't read until after Jon's death his November 1969 letter to George, reporting on afternoons he spent in East Los

Angeles and Watts. "It's come down on us hard now," Jon wrote. "There are twenty different breeds of pigs patrolling every street in the colony here. I mean every section of the city that can be said to be predominately Black is saturated with the establishment's demented gunslingers. . . . Try to get the picture—down every through street they cruise just a few moments apart. . . . Repression is here!" As we studied "The May-Pole of Merry Mount," Hawthorne's arcadian allegory of pleasure and punishment, and *The Great Gatsby*, Fitzgerald's meditation on Jazz Age decadence, in AP English class, Jon offered in another letter to George his own critique of the social order from the Black American perspective our reading list lacked: "The issue of employment is still the same; we do 30 to 40 percent of the nation's work for 1 percent of the returns, and a huge pool of us is always kept unemployed to reduce the value of the labor of those who are, just like 10 years ago, just like 1864–65 when we were thrown on the labor market—hungry, ragged, crowded into clapboards, and unhappy. Nothing has changed since you left the street, comrade, not in this respect at least. Perhaps our condition stands out a little more glaringly, that's all."

A boy from my Unitarian Sunday school, Chris Sutton, had purchased an A. B. Dick motorized mimeograph machine for $100 in the last weeks of August and set it up in the shed behind his house, inviting friends to join him in launching a satirical underground newspaper. The *Pagan Writes* was instantly banned by the school administration but handed out monthly to students by its writers in the park across the street from campus. Chris was in AP English with Jon and me, but even though I'd been editor of the junior high newspaper, I wasn't invited into the *Pagan Writes* clique—all boys. Nor did I write for Blair's student newspaper, the *North Star,* named not for the abolitionist paper founded by Frederick Douglass over a century before, but to honor our school's mascot, the Viking. At McKinley I'd fought with our faculty adviser to publish editorials critical of the school's cafeteria fare and the city's plans to shut down the skating rink where my friend with the JPL-genius father took lessons and the Olympic star Peggy Fleming had trained as a teenager. But by 1969, such causes as a school paper might be allowed to prosecute seemed trivial to me, and the kids who signed up for journalism class too straight.

In those long after-school hours I drifted, instead, into a covert romance with a married graduate student twice my age, who flattered my taste in books and listened when I confided about my father's drinking. Our conversations may have mattered to me more than making out in the front seat of his Chrysler, parked in the shade of towering oaks on side streets near Caltech. But both made me happier than I could remember. Jon's cruising in East LA and Watts brought him after-school thrills; he'd acquired a Browning 9mm and "holed a few" police cars without so far getting caught. "You should see how they'll run when they can't tell from exactly what quarter they're drawing fire," he wrote in his November letter to George, bragging about the officers he'd scared. I also thought I was managing the danger I flirted with, a lovestruck fifteen-year-old with no notion of birth control three years before *Roe.* And maybe I was. It took only one "no" to my paramour's suggestion we find a place to get naked for the nascent affair to end.

Jon quit basketball that winter and started writing for *Iskra,* a political spin-off of the freewheeling, often bawdy *Pagan Writes.* Taking its name from Lenin's prerevolutionary underground paper, *Iskra* ("the Spark") had the support of our chemistry teacher, Lee Browne, founder of a Black community newspaper, the *Pasadena Eagle*. A North Carolinian who'd been refused admission at all-white Duke in the late 1930s and was accepted at the University of Michigan on the condition he live off campus (he refused), Lee Browne ultimately earned his degrees at West Virginia State and NYU, then moved west for a TA position at UCLA. Finding work teaching high school science as a Black man in Southern California in the 1950s took years, but he was never told outright that his rejection was because of race—as was Ruby McKnight Williams, the NAACP chapter president who led the campaign to integrate Brookside Plunge, a generation earlier. Ironically, in Pasadena's tracked classrooms, Mr. Browne taught mostly white students.

Lee Browne was interviewed for *Iskra*'s inaugural issue in February 1970. By then, the Black Panthers Fred Hampton and Mark Clark, men scarcely out of their teens, had been murdered by police in Chicago, Jon's native city. Four days after the killings, a predawn raid of Panther headquarters in Los Angeles, which Jon had certainly passed in his car and may have visited on his tours of the city, provoked a five-hour shoot-out with police, ending in a standoff and multiple injuries and arrests, though no deaths. The Panther resistance was led by nineteen-year-old Wayne Pharr. Lee Browne interpreted this maelstrom for *Iskra*'s student readers: "White Americans with power, it seems, only hear the destructive noises—the riot noises, the assassination noises, the noise of negative mass action. . . . If we don't completely involve black people, other minorities[,] and young dissident people we are programming, computerizing ourselves (America) out of existence." He might have been pleading with his student Jon when he wrote: "Seek meaningful change, work at the decision level."

Jon's first extant contributions to *Iskra* appeared in the second issue, April 1, 1970. In "Racist Educational Structure Attacked," he wrote of the limits of integration at Blair, of being the "only black" in his academic classes except for chemistry, with three Black students out of thirty-two, despite a 23 percent Black enrollment at the school, and of "constantly being bombarded with such questions as, 'Where did you learn that?' and 'Where did you get all this culture?'" accompanied by "the standard incredulous look" from "upper and middle class whites" who, he wrote, "are watching in stunned horror as their balloon of white superiority rapidly deflates with a black spear in its exact center." Knowing full well that *Iskra*'s readers, student editors, and publisher were nearly all white, he closed, "If this letter sounds hostile, it was meant to be. If this letter makes your fur start to bristle, it is time to reevaluate yourself, your ideals and motives. If this letter makes you think I am bitter, you are right." He signed himself "Jonathan Jackson."

Still, at academically—and thereby, in those days, racially—segregated Blair, Jon's school friends were the *Iskra* staff and readers, the white students in his classes. He hung out with them at their homes with backyard pools, hiked and smoked his first joint with them in the Altadena foothills, invited the *Iskra* editors to his house in Northwest Pasadena and showed off the Browning tucked into the waistband of his khakis. "You never know when the Man is going to kick down the door," he explained to his wide-eyed guests. Could Jon's worlds ever have come together?

Jon's bitterness had intensified since February, when his brother was charged, along with two other Black Soledad State

Prison inmates, with pushing a white prison guard out a window to his death. There was no evidence except a connect-the-dots narrative the authorities put forward: three days before, the guard had gunned down three Black prisoners involved in an exercise-yard scuffle, leaving them to die. The guard wasn't disciplined. George was a leader in the Black Guerrilla Family, a resistance effort spreading within California's prisons. The window was near his cell.

In May, Jon and his family traveled north to Monterey County for a pretrial hearing. The young Black UCLA philosophy professor Angela Davis, well-known for her tussle with the university's board of regents over her membership in the Communist Party, was one of the many celebrities—Julian Bond, Pete Seeger, Jane Fonda, Noam Chomsky, Allen Ginsberg—who offered their names in support of a rapidly formed Soledad Brothers Defense Fund. Alone among the famous, Davis joined the Jacksons in the courtroom for the hearing, and she recalled watching the three men enter. "The chains draping their bodies did not threaten us; they were there to be broken, destroyed, smashed," Davis wrote in her 1974 autobiography. "The bile rose in my throat. But more powerful than the taste of outrage was the dominating presence of the Brothers, for the Brothers were beautiful. Chained and shackled, they were standing tall and they were beautiful." In June, Davis visited the Jacksons' home in Pasadena, her late-night arrival waking Jon, who emerged from his bedroom in pajamas, rubbing the sleep from his eyes, Davis remembered.

Jon showed Davis the sheaf of letters from George he kept in the thin brown briefcase he brought to school each day. Some of the letters had already been selected for publication in George's forthcoming book, *Soledad Brother*. But Jon was the first to put any of them into print. The letter he chose for *Iskra*'s final issue of the semester was dated a year earlier, June 16, 1969. George described a fruitless parole hearing, after ten years in prison "for almost nothing"—his role in the theft of seventy dollars. "My 'will' is the thing at issue, they would like to bend me to their will. I've done clean time but this apparently is not enough, they want to see defeat in my eyes before they let me go, I'm expected to enter with bent knee and bowed head." George would not display submission. He went on to advise Jon: "Never settle for less than complete self-determination. . . . It is your obligatory duty as a man to ascertain what is true and worthy, to know what is good for us, and to pursue this against all opposition. . . . [A man] never never even for a second, thinks to abandon the struggle until the final victory is his."

Jon did not print his own letter responding to George's: "Some of us are going to have to take our courage in hand and build a hard revolutionary cadre for selective retaliatory violence." But in *Iskra* Jon added a postscript to his brother's letter: "They couldn't get him that way so they are now trying to crucify him for a murder that he did not commit. If he's bound up tight, I'll hold back the night and there won't be no light for days."

As the school year came to a close we were reading *A Midsummer Night's Dream* aloud in AP English, under the buzzing fluorescent lights of our windowless classroom. Our teacher persuaded Jon to take the role of Pyramus and directed him and another boy, playing Thisbe, to the front of the room to perform Shakespeare's play-within-the-play on the open linoleum between our rows of desks and the blackboard. Our usually quiet classmate became animated, perhaps forgetting for a moment his sadness in the fun of playacting. "Tongue, lose thy light; Moon, take thy flight. Now die, die, die, die, die," Jon read from our Signet Classics paperback in a mock dramatic tenor, and crumpled to the floor, getting laughs. Two months later, he was dead.

IT'S NOT MY place to tell what happened that summer, to raise or attempt to answer the questions that lingered with Jon's classmates and teachers who wished so hard, as the bereaved always do, that it could have gone otherwise and looked for somewhere to place blame. George professed ignorance of Jon's plan, lauding him as the "black man-child with submachine gun in hand," the "*true revolutionary*" who, during the brief span of time he'd controlled the courtroom, "was free for a while. I guess that's more than most of us can expect." Jon's family held no grudge against Angela Davis, despite her link to the weapons he carried. "I knew my son better than anybody," his mother, Georgia Jackson, told an interviewer, "and I know he wouldn't let any woman tell him what to do." There are numerous and sometimes conflicting accounts, from court testimony in Davis's trial to her autobiography, as well as popular and scholarly histories of the Soledad Brothers and Davis cases. Wayne Pharr's biographer, Karin Stanford, is researching a biography of Jonathan Jackson, and greater clarity is sure to come as scholars examine the Davis, Jackson, and Black Panther Party papers archived at Radcliffe's Schlesinger Library, UC Santa Cruz, and Stanford University.

I'd spent the spring semester cocooned in a haze of loneliness, missing my older confidant-beau. Jon's performance as Pyramus is one of my few distinct memories from those months, although that may be the result of the shock we all felt when we heard the news of his fatal hostage-taking scheme. I searched my memory for the day I'd last seen him alive, and that one floated up to become indelible. That and the sight on the TV news of Jon's familiar brown leather briefcase, opened wide in the parking lot of the Marin County Civic Center to reveal cases of ammunition.

There were no public school bereavement counselors in 1970, and when we returned to classes in September, Jon's death went unmentioned by Blair's administration. The message seemed to be that Jon was a criminal now, too dangerous to name even in death. After all, his brother was still at large in the public imagination. Despite George's continued incarceration at San Quentin, his fame spread after the November publication of *Soledad Brother*, with its introduction by Jean Genet. I didn't read the book then—at that age, I'd never bought a newly published book—and I doubt many of my classmates did either. Nor did we discover Julius Lester's rave review in *The New York Times* declaring *Soledad Brother* "one of the most significant and important documents since the first black was pushed off the ship at Jamestown colony. . . . George Jackson makes Eldridge Cleaver look like a song-and-dance man on the Ed Sullivan show." But many others did. The book would go on to sell nearly a half million copies.

I found a boyfriend my own age at school, one of the *Iskra* editors who'd driven up to Oakland for Jon's funeral. A reported three thousand mourners choked the streets outside St. Augustine's Episcopal Church, fists raised, chanting "Power to the People," as Panther pallbearers carried in Jon's coffin along with that of William Christmas, one of the two Black San Quentin inmates also killed in the skirmish. "These brothers didn't have murder on their mind, they had freedom," Huey Newton declared in a eulogy that became a call to arms: "The high tide of revolution is about to sweep the shores of America. . . . Action is supreme!"

Back in Pasadena, I was now part of the clique, as unlikely a member of the white-boy gang as Jon had been. I didn't write for their newspapers, but I joined some of their escapades, the only girl. We got ourselves arrested one night after entering a house of prostitution near the center of town that advertised itself as a health equipment showroom. My boyfriend and his pal wore their letterman jackets; I was in overalls and a black leotard. We chirped our prepared line—"We're pricing equipment for the Blair High School gym"—to the heavily made-up woman at the reception booth, and then to the policeman who'd followed us inside from his squad car, parked for surveillance in front of the building (our tip-off that we had the right place). The cop ordered us back to headquarters, where he booked us for curfew violation, a charge that would vanish from our records when we turned eighteen: white kids let off easy. The prank hadn't been my idea, and I was mortified to have to call my father for a ride home from the station. I couldn't explain what I'd done or why, except I'd wanted to be part of something.

I was glad not to have been invited the night a handful of *Pagan Writes* and *Iskra* kids brought fake tommy guns into a school board meeting to stage a holdup. I can't remember now what cause they hoped to advance—a demand for "open campus" at lunch hour? An end to random locker searches? Or was it simply the bottled-up anger we all felt toward anyone in charge of anything: the disciplinary vice principal, Mr. Pappas, who ordered those searches, whom Jon had excoriated in one of his *Iskra* editorials the year before as "that self styled demagogue and part time dictator Peter 'de Sade' Pappas"; the draft board where some of my male classmates were already registering as they turned eighteen; the College Board and its tests that threatened to determine our futures? The next day in school, my friends didn't tell me what happened after they rushed down the aisles of the auditorium where the meeting was being held, masked and armed with toy weapons. Not much, I guessed. No one was arrested; no one was hurt. The school board members hadn't been fooled.

Were the boys consciously reenacting their friend's lethal gambit in relative safety? No one said so, and I didn't make the connection then myself. Time had speeded up, bearing us away from August 7, 1970, toward graduation and new life ahead. I didn't comprehend, either, the effort at consolation offered by our English teacher when he assigned Faulkner's *Light in August* for reading that year. Did he remember Jon's performance as Pyramus too? Certainly he recognized the tragedy that had befallen his student, caught between two worlds like the biracial Joe Christmas, Faulkner's hero with a name echoing that of Jon's comrade in death, who gave himself up to his brutal murder rather than run. There was a lesson for us I couldn't take in then and still have trouble with now.

Dim as I was about such undercurrents, I'd done well enough in my classes to earn a salutatorian's second-best spot at graduation, which came with the requirement of giving a speech at the school's baccalaureate ceremony the Sunday before commencement. In a way, this was better than coming out on top. The valedictorians of all three Pasadena high schools would give their speeches at one mass rally in the Rose Bowl, where Blair's varsity football team played its home games on Friday nights in the fall. The more expert grade grubbers would hardly be seen, let alone heard, in that setting. At baccalaureate I'd be speaking directly to

my classmates and their families in the school gym, and to that
demagogue Mr. Pappas, certain to be present for the event.

The assigned topic was "True Peace Through Understanding," but I wasn't having it. The school yearbook had just come
out, and as I paged through the senior portraits I discovered that,
although another classmate who'd suffered a brain aneurysm and
died during junior year was pictured with a black border around
his photo, Jon had been left out. His erasure from our school lives
was now complete. I drafted a speech urging my fellow grad-
uating seniors to "live our lives with the personal courage and
conviction and commitment to ourselves of a Jonathan Jackson"
and turned it in for approval. No, I could not give that speech. I
refused to rewrite. My speech was canceled.

The day arrived and I went along to the ceremony anyway,
speech folded into the program I was handed at the door, boyfriend
at my side. We hadn't donned our caps and gowns, hoping to
blend in with the audience, and we took seats among the assem-
bled families in the front row of the bleachers. My name was still
listed in the program, and when the time came, I crossed the gym
floor to the microphone. Alerted to my banishment, the steely Dr.
Wickes, Pasadena's assistant superintendent of schools, rose to
meet me, put her arm around my shoulders, and pulled. My boyfriend's pal, our class president, sprang from the speakers circle and
took hold from the other side, steadying me. I began to speak.

"We are living in an age where anxiety, fear, and frustration
are becoming epidemic. As we watch the destruction of our lands
and waters by a superabundance of pollutants, we feel anxiety. . . .
[A]s we watch the tragic waste of our human resources through
futile wars, through racism, and through our own public system
of mis-education, we feel hopelessness and frustration. There

seems to be no definite road to take, and no base from which to move." Dr. Wickes had returned to her seat, scowling.

I had a recommendation: "We need to become *individuals* who can think and feel and act from the very center of our existence." Was Jonathan Jackson such a person? I wanted to think so. I spoke his name.

I wasn't alone in honoring Jon that June. I look back now through our yearbook and find that the Black Students Union, newly formed, had been founded in memory of Jonathan Jackson and Cecil Jones, the other boy who'd died—"They live on!" Jon's name had made it into the yearbook after all. And my copy of the last issue of the *Pagan Writes* reminds me that Denise Houlemard, homecoming queen, ASB secretary, student senator, member of the 1960 Pasadena Central Library story hour group, had accepted her school service award in her childhood friend's name, also breaching the silence. Jon should have been there. We missed him. We always would.

———

IN LATE AUGUST 1971, I was packing for a flight east to a small, progressive college in Vermont (no grades, pets allowed in dorm rooms, and where a need-based scholarship made attendance cheaper than at California's vaunted public institutions of higher learning) when George Jackson was killed in San Quentin State Prison. Accounts vary here too, but most agree that when a planned prison break involving a handful of inmates was uncovered, George ran into the exercise yard, drawing fire away from the others, sacrificing his own life at age twenty-nine. Three weeks later I was settling into a double room at Bennington College when the Attica Prison Uprising began, fueled by outrage over George Jackson's killing. When, later that fall, a fellow Bennington student knocked on the door of my room, soliciting donations for the Angela Davis Legal Defense Fund—after two months in hiding, she'd been arrested in a New York City motel room and returned to California to face felony charges in abetting Jon's raid—I handed over my few spare dollars. I tried to explain my connection to the cause but couldn't find the words. I'd gotten away. But I still have my "Free Angela" button.

It wasn't until almost a decade later, when I began a career in journalism, that I found reprinted in Jessica Mitford's collection *Poison Penmanship* an interview she'd conducted with George Jackson, first published in *The New York Times Book Review* on June 13, 1971, the same day I'd delivered my salutatorian's speech. Neither Jackson nor Mitford, of course, knew he had only two months more to live—the greatest threat to his life was the uncertain outcome of the Soledad Brothers case—but they spoke as if the now-celebrated author of *Soledad Brother* wasn't facing the electric chair.

Mitford asked about his daily regimen in solitary: "Two or three hours of sleep a day, six hours of exercise, and the rest reading and writing." Writing equipment? Pencil nubs; typewriters not allowed. Literary influences? Here George offered a glimpse of the home life that must have been Jon's too. Georgia Jackson was her elder son's first guide in reading, proffering Wright, Du Bois, Stendhal. At thirteen George read two or three books a week, but "I wanted a life on the street with guys on the block and she wanted me to sit on the couch and read." The result was "a terrible conflict," as mother pressed son toward "black intellectualism" and tried to "assimilate me through the general training of a black bourgeois." Soon George was sneaking out of the house for days at a time. "But while I was home, Mom made me read."

George's conflict with both parents reached Jon through his letters, I learned when I finally read *Soledad Brother* in a yellowed secondhand mass-market paperback edition. Lester Jackson was the prime target: the father who "*pretends* that he is proud of his self-control" when "the guys . . . on his job call him everything under the sun!" George warned Jon: "You must reject his philosophy: the credo of the slave, the self-destructive, self-perpetuating doctrine of the menial, the woodcutter, the waterboy, the groom, the employee, the flunky's flunky, the abased." George counseled a silent rejection and sympathy for Lester: "There are those among us, we must admit, who cannot take any sizable amount of freedom. They are in the majority!" But George himself wasn't silent, writing to Lester, "You have worked hard, hard, and obeyed the laws of our masters but you still have nothing." A house in Pasadena, a salary that covered Catholic school tuition for five children and enabled Georgia to stay home and raise them, urging them all to "read, read, read"—this was nothing?

I don't need to say suspicion of one's elders—anyone over thirty—was endemic to the 1960s. Growing up in Pasadena a few years before Jon, Octavia Butler was a student at Pasadena City College as we entered high school. (Many of my classmates— Mike Dorn, Chris Sutton, Dennis Wun—started college there too.) Butler got her first lessons in Black literature in a PCC night-school class and in Black history from a fellow student who took George's view of the older generation. It was a formative experience, and Butler spoke of it more than once in interviews: listening to "this Black guy saying, 'I wish I could kill all these old Black people that have been holding us back for so long, but I can't because I have to start with my own parents.'" Butler recalled her own anger as a child when she saw her mother enter the houses she cleaned through the back door uncomplainingly, heard the disrespectful words of her mother's employers, and watched her mother's stoic acceptance.

Butler, too, had once believed "the older generation should have rebelled." Yet as she began writing her first novels in the early 1970s and researched the lives of enslaved Black women for the historical fantasy *Kindred*, she changed her mind—her classmate "didn't understand what heroism was." He was "the kind that would have killed and died" instead of "surviving and hanging on and hoping and working for change." Was she thinking of her fellow Pasadenan Jonathan Jackson?

Butler remained in Pasadena for decades, supporting her mother, writing more novels, inventing a proud Black heroine, Lauren Olamina, founder of the Earthseed religion. Butler died of a stroke in 2006 at fifty-eight. Would she have maintained her views if she'd lived to 2020, to witness a new, younger generation's rage over how little has changed? To look back from the distance of half a century on Angela Davis's famous trial and celebrated acquittal in June 1972 is to experience a vertigo no one then could have foretold. What did it all amount to?

After Jon's death, George predicted that an August 7 movement inspired by the example of his brother's martyrdom would lead to armed uprisings around the country, bringing on the full-scale revolution Huey Newton had called for in his eulogy. Instead George was gone a year later, his August death joining Jon's as motivation for the Black August movement, a month-long commemoration of Black resistance fighters stretching back to Nat Turner and his August 1831 rebellion, observed in prison communities and increasingly, in recent years, beyond prison walls. Yet if courage was truly required of anyone, it was Lester and Georgia Jackson, their three daughters, and a grandson, Jonathan P. Jackson Jr., conceived of a summer romance and born eight and a half months after Jon died. All the Jackson brothers' survivors had to learn to live on without them.

———

MY FATHER *HAD* been untrustworthy, even dangerous, when he drove drunk on family vacations in the Sierra Nevada. I was right to leave, although there was nothing courageous in my instinct for survival, my abandonment of a place and people I believed had failed me. But survive I did—too far from home to learn that Lee Browne's house in Northwest Pasadena was razed in the early 1970s as a result of a land grab by wealthy industries at the time of the Pepper Project debacle. He moved to Altadena and dropped "Pasadena" from the title of his newspaper, the *Eagle*. I wasn't there in 1992 when Rodney King's name joined Jackie Robinson's and Octavia Butler's among the "notable alumni" of John Muir High School. I wasn't there in March 2012 when nineteen-year-old Kendrec McDade was killed "in error" by two Pasadena policemen, or in August 2020 when thirty-two-year-old Anthony McClain was fatally shot in the back after a traffic stop as he fled the scene—both within blocks of the original Pepper Project homes.

"I have but one question to ask all of you," Jon wrote in his last editorial for *Iskra*, "What would you do if it was your brother?" Maybe Jon was the hero I wanted him to be. Maybe he had been "free," as George said: he'd carried out his deadly plan not because he believed he had no other choice, but because he had made his choice.

———

Postscript: Jonathan's chemistry class was the last Lee Browne taught at Blair High School. In 1971, he was recruited for a job at Caltech developing a Saturday school and other programs designed to prepare talented public high school students for admission to the rigorous institute. Browne held the position of director of secondary school relations until 1991, when he retired with emeritus status. In November 2021, Caltech's Harry Chandler Dining Hall, named for a former publisher of the Los Angeles Times *known to espouse eugenicist views, was renamed the Lee F. Browne Dining Hall. In making the announcement, college officials noted that in his twenty years of service to Caltech, Browne had successfully "encouraged students from underrepresented backgrounds to consider careers in science."*

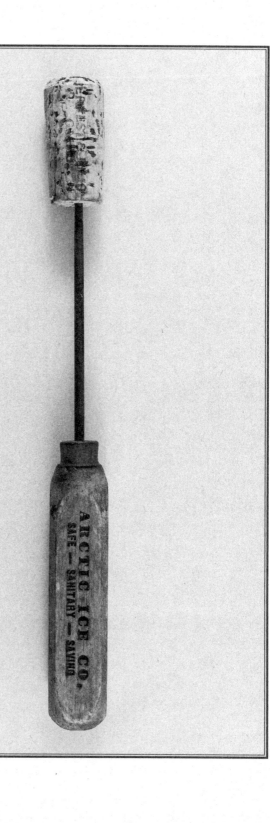

THESE USELESS THINGS

*W*HY DO I KEEP IT? I ask myself each morning. Why do I keep a wooden-handled ice pick on my kitchen window-sill, its tarnished prong thrust into an ancient wine cork for safety's sake? I know I'll never uncork this potentially lethal tool—I have no block of ice in my freezer to chip into slivers to cool a drink. Yet it's the first thing I pause to notice as I look away from the coffee grinder's nagging whir. Why have I kept it and placed it so emphatically *here*?

In truth, I enjoy answering the question as I set down the stilled grinder, take the ice pick's four-sided grip in my hands, and rotate it slowly to admire the alternating black and red inscriptions stamped into its worn planes:

ARCTIC ICE CO. OF LOS ANGELES

LOCALLY OWNED—INDEPENDENT

WE SELL ICE

NO SIDE LINES

ARCTIC ICE CO.

SAFE——SANITARY——SAVING

Phone PArkway 2191

No one else could cherish this battered implement as I do. My grown children would surely toss it if required to sort through their parent's possessions—the task I'd taken on when I claimed the ice pick from my father's overstuffed studio apartment in downtown Arcata, California, after his death in 2008 at age eighty-eight. My daughters have not remarked on the ice pick resting on the windowsill of my own apartment, the one I shared with my partner, Scott, after the end of my marriage until his death in 2019. They may never have seen an ice pick in anyone's hands, except perhaps at a winter carnival featuring ice sculptures. Certainly they never saw this one in my father's hands—the same ones that taught me, on his good days when I was a child, how to hold a hammer and strike a nail, how to draw a saw evenly across a board, how to row a boat. That sometimes disappeared inside a black cloth sack to unload exposed film from a camera by feel.

He held the ice pick in his right hand, the same one that pushed his prized mechanical pencil across a yellow pad as he patiently worked through the steps of long division, of adding and multiplying fractions, to ease my fourth grader's frustration over homework insufficiently explained in my Pasadena elementary school. The ice pick must have come along with the oak ice-cream maker from his childhood home in nearby Altadena. Certainly we never required ice for refrigeration in our own home, would not have contracted with Arctic Ice Co. for delivery, although we subscribed to a milk delivery service during the first few years we lived in Pasadena before my mother went back to work. After that, she left the house too early to retrieve the half dozen milk-filled glass bottles exchanged for the empties waiting in the insulated box I'd grown used to seeing on our shaded back steps on my way to school or outdoors to play. Subscribers or not, on hot summer days we neighborhood kids stood on the curb to flag down the passing milkman and beg him to toss handfuls of ice onto the street—Alta Dena Dairy still relied on ice for cooling in its delivery trucks—where we'd grapple for the biggest shards to suck on, never mind the cold on our fingers. The glistening icicles melted fast on our tongues.

The first step in making ice cream was breaking up the ice. Well, really, the first step was my mother's stirring of milk, eggs, sugar, cream, and vanilla in a saucepan at the kitchen stove the day before, blending the liquid custard that would chill in the ice-cream maker's steel canister overnight in our refrigerator. But that happened out of sight. Can it really be that my dad splintered a block of ice purchased at the gas station up the street with this same wooden-handled pick?

I see him next with hammer raised to strike blows with the flat side of the hammer's head at the burlap sack nestled on the brick patio floor, crushing the frozen fragments trapped inside before pouring the powdery crystals into the wooden bucket, layering ice and rock salt around the custard-filled canister. To anyone who would listen among the kids, cousins, aunts, and uncles gathered for the Fourth of July or a summer birthday celebration, he explained the properties of thermodynamics that would draw the heat out of the liquid, how the slow churning of the dasher would ensure a smooth freeze, the need to keep the salty slush from slopping up the bucket's sides into the sweet ice cream when at last it was firm enough and the crank shaft removed to expose a small hole in the top of the canister where crank met rotating dasher.

Out with the steel canister! Off with its lid and out with the dasher! Patient enough to stay by my father's side through the physics lesson, I was also there to be handed the dasher, allowed to lick away the clotted white remnants clinging to its paddles. A first liquorish taste of vanilla. Then, at last, bowls full of the best ice cream ever made. Or that's the way I remember it.

———

I DON'T REMEMBER living through the developmental stage at which young children explore the world by putting things in their mouths. But it must have been soon after that I discovered the joy of sorting, piling up, forming patterns on the carpet with the objects, no longer useful or just waiting to be used, that my parents offered me for play. There was the plain cedar button box with its exposed corner joinery I still have and open now after years stowed on a bookshelf next to my mother's college texts—music, art history, botany, emblems of her rise to the educated class—to see what's inside. On top, a cluster of yellowing cards bearing sets of three, six, eight buttons of varied sizes and colors from La Mode ("choice of smart women for more than 90 years"), le chic, Jewel-Tone, Pacific, Truecraft, marked with prices ranging from ten to fifty-nine cents. Underneath, a rainbow of discs, the small sea I remember sliding my hands into. I find tiny mother-of-pearl stars and fish; faux brass buttons with eagles and anchors; woven leather buttons that remind me of the hooded camel hair car coat I had in seventh grade and rarely took off, my shelter from high-stress social life in junior high. Sunk to the bottom: a scattering of what appear to be brown and black coffee beans affixed to metal hooks, shoe buttons from a distant age. A crumpled plastic baggie surfaces with the intricate turquoise knots and looped fasteners of the faded Chinese housecoat my mother wore all the years of my childhood as her art-making smock. Why had she saved them when the fabric gave out? Because she had a button box, which became mine after her death, three decades in the past.

What I no longer possess is more vivid still: the cardboard box of ceramic tile samples in muted earth tones, cool to the touch, that I laid out as doll-sized walkways or floors of imaginary rooms on the gray living room rug; the Japanese box whose inlaid rustic scenery split into two and then four cantilevered compartments opening out to reveal bumpy beads of confetti-colored Murano glass and pale carved bone, smooth lozenges of amber, gleaming pink crystal globes with miniature explosions inside—my grandmother's broken jewelry. I never thought of the kitchens or bathrooms the tiles might have lined, the neck-laces from which the beads had come unstrung. These useless things had no past or future; they were simply mine to handle and admire, in a way, to love.

And then I learned to read. Words carried me away from things, even as things brought me to words: "A Apple pie." The irritating simplicity of abecedarian picture books signaled that wisdom lay elsewhere. Things were a way station. Quickly I was beyond them. I looked forward to the end of the school day so I could rejoin the characters in whichever book waited for me half read on my bed. If my books were illustrated, I rapidly turned the page, unwilling to have my private visions disturbed or the plot stalled. On weekends I had to be coaxed to play outside, where once I'd happily gathered acorns beneath the live oak that dominated our front yard, made mud pies piled high with fronds rudely stripped from the ferns in my mother's garden. Now, though I'd never once seen snow fall, I felt the cold of Heidi's Alp, of the White Witch's Narnia. I believed I could taste the grandfather's healthful goat's milk, Edmund's coveted Turkish delights; consumed in my imagination, the supply would never run out. With Meg Murry, I could put on Mrs. Who's magic eyeglasses and travel through icy outer space to save my family.

I DETERMINED TO be a writer, and through the words of others I made my way in the profession. The work of biography seemed invented for me: I could sit for days and months, then years, in library archives deciphering the handwritten letters and diaries of my subjects, hearing them speak to me across the centuries, entering their thoughts into my notes and finally, back home, into my books.

I specialized at first in lesser-known female intellectuals, voracious readers like me. One editor advised me to include details of how they dressed and what they ate. "Readers like that," she said. But my insistently cerebral women rarely wrote about food or clothing. There was the famous "all-day party" at Ralph Waldo Emerson's Concord home in September 1837 after he'd delivered the "American Scholar" address, his ode to the "active soul," at

Harvard College's commencement. This was the first meeting of the Transcendental Club—an intimate "symposium" of disaffected Unitarian ministers augmented by Henry David Thoreau and Bronson Alcott—to which women were invited, at least in part because Emerson's wife, Lidian, had been conscripted to provide nourishment: a "noble great piece" of beef, a leg of mutton, cucumbers, tomatoes, lettuce, applesauce, and rice pudding with currants, she recorded in a letter. Margaret Fuller had been there, and two years later she led the conversation at a small party in a brick row house on Boston's Beacon Hill, attended by Nathaniel Hawthorne and his fiancée, Sophia Peabody, at which "preserved Greek roses" and oranges were served. Sophia, an artist and sometime invalid, adhered to a diet of boiled rice and milk when she was unwell. But that was it for food.

As for clothing, I discovered that when Mary Peabody—the middle of the three sisters to whom I devoted my first book— wrote to the eldest sister, Elizabeth, that she'd bought a dress in Boston, she meant she'd acquired a *length of cloth* that would be *made into* a dress. Laundering clothes was a cumbersome task, undertaken infrequently. To freshen up a dress, detachable collars made of white cotton or linen and sometimes trimmed with lace were alternated; these could be washed and ironed more frequently. The editor had been right: the difference between the Peabody sisters' homespun world and my ready-made one hit home with details like these. Reading a biography of their friend Emerson, I was charmed to learn that, around the time they all became acquainted, the thirtysomething philosopher "carried his money in an old wallet wrapped in twine." Though fluent— perhaps overly fluent—in abstraction, Emerson claimed to prefer the material to the verbal: "The thing set down in words is not (thereby) affirmed."

Still, when a fellow researcher in the archives of the Massachusetts Historical Society stood up from a nearby table and broke the reading room's silence with a gasp of wonder—he'd just opened a small box containing the bracelet of gold beads once strung on a necklace worn by Elizabeth Freeman, whose 1781 court case helped bring an end to slavery in Massachusetts—I paused only a moment to witness his joy, then returned to the manuscripts on my desk. I'm not sure which letter or diary page I was reading that day. It could have been Mary Peabody's recollection of the moment when her future husband, the reformer and politician Horace Mann, first smiled at her across the boardinghouse dinner table they shared, and "I felt the glow permeate every fibre & vein." Or Elizabeth Peabody's letter to Mary from the time of that meeting: "I can get food for my mind in books—in observation of life—in my own reflections, [but] food for my heart must come direct from others—& *my heart* always craved more than my mind." Mary worried that Elizabeth, her roommate in the same boardinghouse, had fallen in love with Horace Mann too.

I was lucky, even as the thousands of closely written pages I would ultimately peruse stretched my project from the contractual three years to twenty: lucky to have so many revelatory words as evidence of my subjects' interior lives. Around the time I began my research in the mid-1980s, the profession of history was embarking on what's since been termed the "material turn" away from documents and toward objects as vehicles for telling the stories of people who, like Freeman, couldn't write or whose lives passed unremarked in archival records. Key to the practice of material culture studies is the notion that objects are themselves repositories of information that can be interpreted as evidence of the past. As the Yale art historian Jules Prown writes in *Art as Evidence*, "There is a language of form as there is a language of words; a naming through making as there is a naming through saying"—or writing.

Archaeologists and historical anthropologists had been mining this vein for decades, seeking ways to conjure up the spirits of past civilizations by means of excavated artifacts. Now historians began to study items held in archives that had once been considered decorative or quaint, the province of collectors and "antiquarians"—textiles, furniture, cooking utensils, tableware— as measures of the values of the societies in which they'd been produced and prized. Did the curves of a pewter teapot made during the American Revolution communicate a longing, in that tumultuous time, for maternal warmth and nurture—a safety threatened by separation from the mother country, England? Even texts could be seen as objects. Old books were of interest for the ways they were used as much as for their content: Had readers underlined passages or scribbled in the margins, spilled coffee or wine or semen on their pages?

History, and soon biography, could be narrated with the aid of or exclusively through the examination of *things*. Neil Mac-Gregor's *A History of the World in 100 Objects* led the way for Deborah Lutz's *The Brontë Cabinet: Three Lives in Nine Objects*, which brought Charlotte, Emily, and Anne Brontë's lives into focus by way of a walking stick, a pair of slippers, and a dog collar, among other treasures. In *All That She Carried: The Journey of Ashley's Sack, a Black Family Keepsake*, Tiya Miles derived a multigenerational saga from a simple cotton bag embroidered with a family history distilled into just fifty-three neatly stitched words, the largest of which was "Love."

WERE WORDS EVER enough? I'd hurried past the things that came with the words, and now they reappeared to tease my imagination. During the years before the three Peabody sisters had been separated from one another in marriage, they often teamed up as schoolteachers or in publishing ventures. I'd found a relic of one such collaboration, a rare copy of *Primer of Reading and Drawing* written by Mary in 1841, published by Elizabeth, and illustrated, most likely, by the youngest sister, the artist Sophia. I hadn't given the drawing exercises much thought when I first discovered the book in an archive in the 1980s; I was captivated instead by Mary's unusual method of teaching reading, which emphasized the comprehension of whole words and phrases extracted from allegorical tales printed in the book: "the silent thought in the soul," "the tenderness of conscience," "the beauty of truth."

I remembered the sketches now, and how the everyday objects and structures presented in outline for students to copy on their slates had seemed unfamiliar, even unrecognizable, to me. I could guess at the warming pan, marvel at a domed lighthouse and a steeply sloped shingled roof. I had to consult a research librarian at Old Sturbridge Village, a re-created 1830s town in central Massachusetts open to tourists, to identify what appeared to be an extra-tall fire hydrant with a handcart leaning against it: a hitching post. I'd walked the brick sidewalks and cobblestone streets of Boston and Salem where the Peabody sisters once lived, picturing my subjects striding along in full skirts and bonnets. But I'd failed to consider the bustle of commerce around them, the horse-drawn wagons and carriages, the shouts of drivers and tradesmen, the stench of manure—all of which were called up by the mystifying sketch of a hitching post that schoolchildren of the 1840s would have known on sight. A curious sort of four-legged stool without a seat turned out to be a stand on which a keg of molasses or rum might rest in a kitchen or pantry. When was the last time anyone had kept a keg of molasses at the ready in an American kitchen? Or an icebox?

Obsolescence may be the fate of most man-made things, even as many objects outlast their owners, like my father's ice pick. The simple device, sitting idle on my windowsill, bespeaks a history both larger and longer than one man's singular nine-decade lifespan—and very nearly lost. Not only is the implement itself outmoded, but the commercial enterprise that once made an ice pick ubiquitous as a tool, and, in the first half of the twentieth century, a means of advertisement for local purveyors of blocks of ice for household use, has all but vanished.

The ice trade, begun on the frozen lakes and ponds of New England, was well established by the time the Peabody sisters published their *Primer.* In *Walden,* their friend Thoreau wrote of witnessing a one-hundred-man crew of Irish immigrants arrive with their "Yankee overseers" each day in the depths of winter 1846–47 to "get out the ice" from Walden Pond. The process was as familiar to him as it is foreign to me:

> They divided it into cakes by methods too well known to require description, and these, being sledded to the shore, were rapidly hauled off on to an ice platform, and raised by grappling irons

and block and tackle, worked by horses, on to a stack, as surely as so many barrels of flour, and there placed evenly side by side, and row upon row, as if they formed the solid base of an obelisk designed to pierce the clouds.

That winter's harvest, estimated at ten thousand tons of ice, was insulated with hay and covered with boards for storage on Walden's banks until the following July, when the blocks were carted off to Boston's wharves for shipment in the dank holds of merchant vessels. "Thus it appears that the sweltering inhabitants of Charleston and New Orleans, of Madras and Bombay and Calcutta, drink at my well," Thoreau mused in his one-room shelter. "The pure Walden water is mingled with the sacred water of the Ganges."

With the advent of chemical refrigerants late in the nineteenth century, the commingling of distant waters came to an end. Ice could be made, rather than harvested, and eventually the great blocks were no longer needed. One hundred years after *Walden*, when John Updike, the twentieth-century author most indebted to the Concord circle, wrote the first of his *Rabbit* novels, the defunct ice trade became an "objective correlative," in T. S. Eliot's phrase, for the nostalgic mood that would link all four books, written at ten-year intervals over three decades. As Eliot understood, *things* are what make fiction, poetry, drama, and the emotions they stir, feel real, true.

In *Rabbit, Run*, a novel of the 1950s published in 1960, twenty-six-year-old Harry "Rabbit" Angstrom, married and a father, but scarcely employable in the town where he once starred in high school basketball games, marks his distance from youthful acclaim each time he passes the "deserted ice plant with its rotting wooden skids on the fallen loading porch." The gutter where the "slime-rimmed ice-plant water used to run is dry." Yet in his dreams, Harry can still conjure up the "wood icebox" in the "old kitchen" of his childhood home, and a girl at the table stretching her long arm to open the icebox door, revealing "the square cave where the cake of ice sits." Cold air rushes out, "and there it is, inches from Harry's eyes, lopsided from melting but still big, holding within its semi-opaque bulk the white partition that the cakes have when they come bumping down the chute at the ice plant." The dreaming Harry leans closer to see that "under the watery skin are hundreds of clear white veins like the capillaries on a leaf, as if ice too were built up of living cells. And further inside, so ghostly it comes to him last, hangs a jagged cloud, the star of an explosion. . . . The rusted ribs the cake rests on wobble through to his eyes like the teeth of a grin. Fear probes him; the cold lump is alive." Harry's past is alive to him, but receding with the melting ice.

In *Rabbit Redux*, the icebox and its menacing lump are forgotten in the chaotic late '60s, an era of rapid modernization indifferent to Harry Angstrom: The refrigerator "speaks to itself, drops its own ice into its own tray." But a decade later, the ice plant reappears in *Rabbit Is Rich*, when the suddenly prosperous Harry takes up jogging. On the "homeward leg" of his route he passes "the gutter where the water from the ice plant used to run," notices "an edge of green slime," and observes, as a latter-day Thoreau might, "Life tries to get a grip anywhere." The sight reminds Harry of a morning in boyhood when, "clowning on the way to school," "he slipped on the slime and fell in, got his knickers soaked, those corduroy knickers they used to make you wear." The recollection transports Harry back to that day and prompts a host of further memories that evoke "a strange sort of peace," as surely as the taste of a madeleine dipped in lime-flower tea recalled Proust to his blissful childhood in the French countryside. In the final novel in the series, *Rabbit at Rest,* the slime is gone from the long-dry gutter, but "the cement was permanently tinged green." Fifty-five years old, recovering from a first heart attack and soon to die of a second, Harry thinks, as he takes a last turn—walking, not running now—past the familiar intersection: "Something tragic in matter itself, the way it keeps watch no matter how great our misery."

Although a full generation younger than John Updike, I, too, grew up with a wooden icebox, used on summer vacations to cool milk and other perishables in the one-room mountain cabin my family of five shared with my maternal grandparents, uncle and aunt, and their five children—trading off weeks and sometimes overlapping for a few days of happy tumult. I recognize the exploding star Updike described, trapped in the center of the dwindling block of ice my father had lugged up the trail from the pier to lower into the top compartment of the oak chest, new when the log cabin was built in the 1930s and effective through the years of my childhood.

And there is my father once more, in a memory prompted by a *thing.* Yes, I still see the icebox every time I visit the cabin; it's used now to store paper goods, since we acquired a secondhand propane-fueled fridge sometime in the 1970s. None of us grown cousins can bear to part with the memories called forth by the oak chest, its surface still glossy from our grandmother's regular shellackings. In an article titled "Beyond Words," the historian Leora Auslander writes of "the continued existence of intimately used objects" after the deaths of their owners and the special power of things to give substance to memories: "a dematerialized memory is both very fragile and also less satisfying to human beings— who are, after all, of flesh and blood." Little wonder that therapists who treat hoarders warn their decluttering patients, "Don't pick it up!" When holding my father's ice pick, opening the lid of the ice chest, our hands meet. How could I throw or give away either of these "mortal" objects, as Auslander terms the things that outlive their owners?

Do the objects that survive from our childhoods, useless except as aids to memory, bear witness to our ongoing lives, as Updike suggests? Had I placed my father's ice pick on my pantry windowsill to keep watch over me, as a father might? But my father wasn't that sort of dad. I hadn't tossed out the high school class president's gavel inscribed with his name that he'd received in 1938, or the prize book he'd been awarded at Harvard for good grades in his freshman year the following spring; but I stored them away where I'd never have to look at them. I didn't want to be reminded of his failed promise. In *The Centaur,* Updike's most autobiographical novel, he writes of the rare occasions when the young protagonist's disappointed and disappointing dad "handled himself with the deftness, the expertness that is, after all, most of what we hope for from fathers." When wielding the ice pick, my father *was* the father I hoped for. And perhaps the implement's concealed danger, the spike blunted with a wine cork, spoke to me of my father as well. I had him in hand on the windowsill.

I COULD TELL you how, half expecting to hear a voice from the distant past, I started to dial the phone number on the Arctic Ice Co. ice pick—only to realize that, even after adding the central Los Angeles area code, 213, there weren't enough digits to make the call. And how Arctic's two-letter, four-digit number—PArkway 2191—dated the ice pick back to before 1947, when two letters and *five* numbers were mandated nationwide, which reminded me of the great debate of 1963, the year I turned nine, over "all-number calling" (ANC), and how ultimately, despite a suit filed by the celebrity lawyer Melvin Belli on behalf of the ADDLSF (Anti-Digit Dialing League of San Francisco), I had to say a wistful goodbye to my own SYcamore exchange. I could tell how I resorted to Google and found a conglomerate, Arctic Glacier Premium Ice, whose pale blue snowy-peak logo I recognized from the plastic bags of ice cubes I used to buy when I gave big parties, back when I was married and lived in a large enough house. And how I wondered whether tiny Arctic Ice Co. at 1615 Cordova—one of thirty-one neighborhood ice distributors listed in the 1936 Los Angeles Yellow Pages, digitized by the Library of Congress—could have morphed into one of North America's three largest ice manufacturers, capable of delivering 2.5 billion pounds of ice annually. Arctic Glacier offers ice sculptures, dry ice, and artificial snow as well as bagged, crushed, and block ice in quantities large enough for corporate events, gala weddings, and disaster relief. But Arctic Glacier's history, touted online, dashed my hopes: founded in Winnipeg in 1882, Canada's Arctic Ice Company made its last home delivery in 1954, the year I was born, and subsequently embarked on the relentless acquisition of independent local and regional companies, rebranding as Arctic Glacier in 1996 and entering the U.S. market the following year. A sampling of names from the list of twenty-seven family-owned ice delivery businesses swallowed up by Arctic Glacier since 2017 would make a poignant elegy: Astoria, Emerald, Mountain, Rose, Avalanche, Creed, Gem, Hawkeye, Blue Sky. The latest to succumb is Brookline Ice Company, operated by the Signore family for nearly one hundred years just across the Charles River from the apartment where my father's ice pick rests on a windowsill.

Here's the story I'd rather tell. I receive an email from a realtor in Haverford, Pennsylvania. His wife has been reading my book, the one about the Peabody sisters. "I picked it up, was entranced," he writes. "The scene is quite familiar to me. I was born in Boston and lived in Concord."

More than the scene was familiar to him. On page 170 of *The Peabody Sisters,* he read about "a handsome writing desk," given to the two older sisters, Elizabeth and Mary, by their students at the end of the 1826 summer term, stocked with writing paraphernalia, including sealing wax and "a seal with a heart upon it," bearing the motto "You merit it." This was the first school the sisters opened together, at ages twenty-one and eighteen, and they were leaving under a cloud after just fifteen months. Elizabeth's experimental teaching style angered the parents. The gift, and especially the motto, assured the sisters they had done no wrong.

"I believe I own that 'desk,'" he writes to me, "actually a writing box, with a brass plate imbedded on the cover with E.P. and M. T. Peabody 1826 engraved on it." The seal with its consoling motto is no longer in the box, only "some bits of wax residue," he is careful to add. "No one in my family has the slightest interest in owning this treasure," he writes, "and, as part of reducing our household inventory, I would like to sell it." Similar antique writing boxes usually sell for two hundred dollars, he notes, and "there doesn't appear to be a very deep market." Considering the history, this one might fetch more.

I try brokering a sale for him with the curators I know, but the inscription, even with the correct year of gift and precise initials (the sisters' full names are Elizabeth Palmer Peabody and Mary Tyler Peabody), isn't enough to satisfy. He is unable to trace the writing box's lineage directly back to the Peabody family. Reader, I buy it. Three hundred dollars for a Honduran mahogany portable writing desk handcrafted in England at the turn of the nineteenth century; I determine, as I look back through the sisters' correspondence, that the desk cost fifteen dollars in 1826—about four hundred in today's currency.

"I am writing on a writing desk which was presented to Mary and me by our scholars," Elizabeth begins a letter from Brookline, Massachusetts, to her sister Sophia in Salem on August 14, 1826, one hundred years before the founding of Brookline Ice, nearly two hundred years before the desk becomes mine. "It is one of the handsomest I ever saw." She itemizes the contents—"Everything convenient for writing"—and I attempt to visualize. These are more than words to me now: "paper, wafers, ink stand, sand stand, a pen-knife which cost a dollar, an ivory knife to cut paper with, a silver pencil case with pencil in it." Wafers? Tiny, colorful rounds of paste, ready-made for sealing. Sand stand? I remember learning that wet ink could be blotted with a scattering of sand. Penknives are still sold today, yet it hasn't occurred to me until this moment that they once had a function related to pens: shaping quills, still the most common writing implements in the 1820s, when metal fountain pens were new to the market.

"This was accompanied by a note (very affectionate) which I shall bring home to show you," Elizabeth continues. The students, teenaged girls, collected the funds by "subscription" over two months, keeping the gift a surprise until the last day of school, when they hid it in the sisters' attic bedroom, upstairs from the sitting room that doubled as a classroom, to be discovered by their happy teachers. "How delightful it is this overflowing heart of the young. How blest is the employment which brings one in such close contact with it," Elizabeth wrote in her journal that night. The gift is all the more remarkable, I know, because one year earlier, at the close of the school's first term, Elizabeth handed each student a personal letter containing a frank, critical assessment of her character. The "impression" on the seal she used then was "a lancet—I wound to heal." Elizabeth spent that summer holiday consumed with worry. Had she been too hard on them? But when school resumed in September, "they were all quiet and grave—but affectionate," and she received "a good many" notes from the girls, "grateful—& full of good resolutions."

He will arrive by car from Pennsylvania, after dropping his wife at her college reunion in a Boston suburb. I give directions, but he explains by email that he will not take the Mass Pike; he'd rather follow Trapelo Road all the way to my apartment, the route he remembers from childhood, when the busy street was traversed by "electrified trolleys, complete with overhead rails and a motorman." The intersection closest to my apartment, still known as Cushing Square, was referred to by locals back then as "cushion square," he informs me, and "quite upscale, anchored by SS Pierce (pronounced *purse*), a purveyor of delicacies and fine wines." Now there's a gas station, a Starbucks, and a UPS store.

He's late and a bit flustered. The traffic was slow and Trapelo Road lacked the familiar landmarks. He places the box carefully on the clean towel I've laid out on my kitchen table, and I'm humbled by how little I knew when I wrote about a portable writing desk without having seen one.

It *is* a box, eighteen inches wide, nine inches deep, and six high. So much more thrilling than my mother's simple cedar button box, though not much larger, its richly grained toffee-brown surface, delicate brass bindings, and recessed handle suggest treasure. When I lift the lid, I see how it's angled so that when the box is fully open, a slanted writing surface is formed, lined in worn black velvet. This desk has been much used. Compartments, now empty, designed to hold all the items on Elizabeth's list appear, along with grooved slots for storing pencils and pens. A slender metal pin with an eye-hook, when lifted, frees up a secret drawer, impossible to access when the box is closed. But of course it is the inscription on the brass plate, the Peabody name and the sisters' initials engraved in flowing script reminiscent of their own handwriting, that draws me back—as if I'd been there with them!—and moves me to tears.

After he leaves, I close the box and place it on a shelf I've cleared over my desk. There is no seal waiting inside to tell me, when I need consolation, "You merit it." That message was intended for Elizabeth and Mary Peabody anyway. But the realtor from Haverford, Pennsylvania, writes the next day in response to my emailed thanks: "I am so pleased that the box has a home that it deserves!" I have come full circle—acquiring a *thing* that represents, may even have produced, the words I so cherished in writing the sisters' lives.

The Peabody sisters' writing desk will outlast my father's ice pick, which is sure to be consigned to the rubbish heap soon after my own demise, if not before, should I one day face a move to smaller quarters. Maybe I'll start in on the search for an archive or historical museum that will accept my certainty about the mahogany box's origins and take it off my hands when I'm ready to part with it. But that won't be for a long time.

For now I'm happy to set my morning cup of coffee down next to my own portable writing device—a Lenovo IdeaPad S340 laptop computer, which also opens to reveal secrets, to enable me to reveal mine—and look up at the shelf where the most "handsome" and efficient writing box of its kind in 1826 reminds me of my purpose. The box may not be used, but it is not useless to me. If Jules Prown is right and there is a language of form, my two portable "desks," each containing "everything convenient" in one compact case, speak of the enduring human need to communicate in writing, to give *things* life in words.

是より約250M

鴨長明方丈石

WITHOUT

MOST MORNINGS THIS FALL I walk for nearly an hour in my neighborhood of two-family houses in a Boston suburb, following a set route, an extension of the daily walks I used to take with my aging golden retriever, Rudy, gone three years last spring: up several blocks to the playing field with its soccer pitch and twin Little League diamonds, then a wide loop around a dozen more blocks, across a busy road, and up the hill to circle the town reservoir, before turning back home. Without my beloved partner, Scott, gone more than a year now, I walk to ease nagging back pain and to escape the first-floor apartment where I'm otherwise confined under COVID-19 restrictions in a dizzying aloneness, extreme bereavement. I nod and wave to other masked walkers, joggers, and cyclists, none of whom I know. I did not raise my children in this neighborhood.

Flowering dogwoods, lilac hedges, and star magnolias embellished the late New England spring. In summer I watched for new blooms, peonies and iris giving way to roses and lilies, in the several well-tended gardens along my route; most homeowners here content themselves with squares of lawn and a bit of shrubbery, an azalea or rhododendron.

When was it I began to see in my mind's eye, as I paced my accustomed path, the narrow streets, low wooden and stucco houses, and storefronts of Nishifukunokawa-chō, the Kyoto neighborhood where I'd lived for three autumn months almost three years ago? Some autonomic response triggered by my pacing feet and the nodding strangers must have flashed glimpses of the fruit seller, organic grocer (from whom I could buy a single fresh egg the day it was laid), fishmonger, public bath, and bento box restaurant I passed on the main street leading to or from the university campus where I was posted that semester, then the barber pole signaling my turn into a network of domestic alleyways (no lawns, plenty of potted succulents), past the sandlot playground of the elementary school, to my door—a sliding wooden panel in a centuries-old single-story timber structure that I released by punching a series of numbers on a keypad.

I arrived in Kyoto in late August 2017, knowing almost nothing about the city or the country of which it had once been the capital. I was the guest of a professor of American literature at Kyoto University, and my qualifications for the fellowship I'd earned had nothing to do with Japan. My duties were simply to deliver several lectures on the New England transcendentalist women who were the subjects of my first two biographies, attend an occasional graduate seminar, and advise the few graduate students in American literature whose spoken English was strong enough to enable conversation. (The Japanese educational system provides little opportunity for study abroad in the humanities.) Otherwise

I was at liberty to pursue my research on Nathaniel Hawthorne's novels and their heroines in my drab but capacious office down the hall from the graduate students' shared workspace, or wherever I chose, as long as I stamped in on the logbook at department headquarters each day with the orange *hanko* seal presented to me by my host, Professor Naoyuki Mizuno, a Henry James specialist. Hence my repeated walks to and from campus.

Over lunch in the weeks before I left, a friend back in Boston, a retired professor of Asian art, had pressed two volumes on me— *The Tale of Genji* and *The Pillow Book of Sei Shōnagon,* in Arthur Waley's translations—and sketched for me the general outlines of the Heian period (794–1185 CE), when the Fujiwara dynasty cultivated a refined aesthetic that supported these first great works of Japanese literature, both written by women of the court. (High-status men of the time clung to the stilted idioms derivative of the Chinese characters, *kanji,* used in formal Japanese writing, leaving women to develop a modern vernacular style using the newer phonetic *kana.*) But I hadn't packed the books in my suitcase. I hadn't packed any books in my suitcase or even in my carry-on bag. I'd recently injured my back while piling up boxes of research materials from past writing projects to put into storage and was worried about reinjury on the long flight.

Without anything to read as the plane bumped and heaved itself into open airspace, I rehearsed in my mind the two poems I knew by heart: Robert Frost's "Stopping by Woods on a Snowy Evening," memorized in fifth grade when I thought I wanted to be a poet, and "One Art," the famous villanelle on "the art of losing" by Elizabeth Bishop, my onetime professor whose biography I'd just finished writing in a book that also recounted my failure to follow through on that early ambition. Never mind the long-ago failure. I was on my way to a residence in a foreign land, the sort of adventure I'd always longed for and that Elizabeth Bishop, an ardent traveler, would surely have approved. And to a period of radical isolation I could not have known would prepare me for now.

———

IT WOULD BE inaccurate to say I'd come to Kyoto University for the fall semester. I was *leaving* my American college for the fall semester. Offered the chance to spend three months on KU's campus, I'd requested September through November; Scott liked to vacation in the fall and could leave work to join me for ten days in October. Politeness, I suppose, had prevented Professor Mizuno from informing me that the university would be closed during the entire first month of my stay. Japanese semesters run from April through August, October through February, with a full month off for cherry blossom festivals in March. Classes wouldn't start until October 5, I learned that first day, and none of the professors or graduate students I'd corresponded with in advance lived in Kyoto. They all commuted on Japan's excellent rapid transit system from distant suburbs or other cities in the Kansai region, which encompassed Osaka, Nara (another former national capital), and several smaller municipalities. I was on my own in this foreign city, where I couldn't even make out street signs, let alone the packaging on products I might want to buy in the local convenience store. Which carton was milk? Which container held plain yogurt?

Professor Mizuno—a mustached man of about my height

and exactly my age, he informed me, having handled the many documents necessary for my appointment as visiting professor— stayed to give me a tour of the campus, showing off its central plaza with clock tower and massive, iconic camphor tree, the latter as old as the dilapidated warren of dark wooden dormitory buildings he pointed out, erected in 1897 at the university's founding. These were the last original structures on campus, recently condemned by KU authorities as unsafe, but still occupied by a band of student holdouts whose protest signs dotted the campus, undecipherable by me.

Professor Mizuno bought me a ream of printer paper and a handful of pens at the campus store and, when we ended the tour at his cluttered office, where books in English and Japanese stood two-deep on the shelves lining the room, offered reassurance about the specter of nuclear war that had suddenly intruded on our lives. On the morning of August 29, as my Japan Airlines flight winged its way toward Tokyo, North Korea had lobbed a test ICBM in a seventeen-hundred-mile arc passing over the northern Japanese island of Hokkaido. Throughout Japan, citizens were ordered to shelter in place until the missile was observed to splash down in an empty stretch of the Pacific.

I had nothing to worry about in Kyoto, Professor Mizuno told me. If North Korea were to bomb Japan, the targets would surely be the American military installations in Tokyo or Okinawa, he said. This was consolation? As for the tantruming tyrants deciding our fates, Kim Jong Un and Donald Trump, then just seven months into his first year in office—"Crazy," he judged them, and shrugged his shoulders. What could anyone do?

Professor Mizuno's fatalism may have been cultural, but it

was also learned. Some weeks later, when we met again over pizza in a sleek trattoria near campus, he told me about his uncle Susumu, pilot of a *shinyo*, the naval equivalent of a kamikaze plane, whose life had been spared by the bombing of Hiroshima and Nagasaki. On receiving his assignment to the *shinyo* fleet, Susumu Mizuno had considered himself dead; but the war ended before the scheduled date of his suicide mission. My KU host grew up hearing his uncle refer to the natural span of years he was in the end permitted to live as his "afterlife."

That night, stretched out on the futon I'd unfurled on tatami in my tiny habitation, I fell asleep reciting the poems I'd practiced on the flight, conjuring Frost's icy resolve, Bishop's charm against loneliness, in the formless humid darkness. I still had no books. My iPhone ran on a Japanese data plan whose midnight alarms a few days later, when the first of three equinoctial typhoons swept through Kyoto, spoke in a foreign tongue and delivered text messages in enigmatic characters. What dangers I'd been warned of, I never knew.

———

KU'S STUDENT A CAPPELLA groups and baseball team were in residence on campus, rehearsing American pop songs in outdoor corridors, snapping fingers and breaking into dance moves, taking batting practice on the dusty field that occupied one large corner of South Campus where my office and a handful of classroom buildings stood, along with a small undergraduate library, open but empty of patrons, and the squatter-filled dorms. Chickens pecked in the weeds outside a coop near the dorms, behind several rows of empty bicycle racks. I saw few adults.

An American friend's Japanese aunt kindly took the *shinkan-sen* in from Nagoya, about an hour's ride; treated me to a *kaiseki* lunch (half the price of a similar multicourse dinner; I quickly learned to make lunch my main meal); and introduced me to the subway. But after that first trip I rarely went back underground. Unable to make out words on signs or informational placards at train stations, museums, temples, shrines, or restaurants, I was experiencing a species of blindness—the written cues that might have allowed me to make sense of my environment were illegible—which heightened my desire to *see*.

I fetched copies of Hawthorne's four novels from the undergraduate library, itself no easy task: books were shelved on the British system, by date of acquisition within an author's oeuvre, rather than alphabetically by title. I forced myself to spend an hour or so each day reading in my office or a coffee shop, or over my ample lunch. But the visual occlusion I suffered seemed to extend to English words too. I didn't want to read, could no longer summon the concentration that had kept me at my desk or in the archives as I researched and wrote three biographies in as many decades.

I walked for miles up the road bordering the Kamo River to a home goods store in search of a spare pillow for Scott's October visit, astonished by the ribbon of wild water cutting through the city. Egrets and gray herons stalked its shallows; fishermen in waders cast their rods. Hurtling in its broad course, churning up white water as it passed over rocky beds, the Kamo was nothing like the placid Charles back home, or the majestic Thames, Seine, or Tiber I'd seen on European travels. I was still more astonished to discover the chains of broad stepping stones, blocks of concrete cast in the shapes of turtles and fish, spanning the river at regular intervals, inviting pedestrians to cross without resorting to heavily trafficked bridges. I watched intrepid adults with packages and briefcases in their hands and schoolchildren in uniforms and caps bearing hefty backpacks leap from stone to stone, judging for themselves whether passage was safe. When I saw how high the water rose the day after that first typhoon, submerging the stepping stones in a roaring torrent, I guessed that had been the message on my cell phone: *Stay away from riverbanks.*

I walked to temples and house museums with elaborate gardens, but rarely ventured indoors. One of Kyoto's prime tourist sites, a full-scale replica of the Heian Palace where Genji had once intrigued and Sei Shōnagon wrote in her pillow book, was just a few blocks from my tiny house. (Many palaces and temples I visited, ancient as they appeared, had been painstakingly and repeatedly reconstructed over the centuries after fires partially or fully consumed their wooden frames.) I'm sure my art historian friend would have taken the Heian Palace tour, but I wasn't interested, and the guides were nowhere in evidence the day I first wandered onto the grounds. Another typhoon was forecast. No tour buses lined the street in front of the palace's extravagant gates; the vast interior courtyard was nearly empty of people. Thrilling clouds filled the sky over the orange-timbered great hall. The wind picked up, blowing the strips of white cloth representing wishes, tied to the branches of two small trees growing near the hall's entrance, in fascinating whorls. I realized, to my surprise, I felt safe, knowing I was just a few minutes' walk from home. I left and walked there, stopping to buy a flashlight at the convenience store in case of a power outage that never came.

FAR INTO SEPTEMBER, still lacking companionship, I looked up
the ex-girlfriend of a lifelong friend of mine, an Indian architect
with a talent for amicable breakups. He had former girlfriends
all over the globe, it sometimes seemed, all of them brilliant,
offbeat, and friendly to him still. This one was an American
who'd moved to Japan thirty years ago and stayed there, marrying and raising a family in a village outside Kyoto, training
as a Noh player and eventually joining a professional troupe, a
rarity for a woman, let alone a non-Japanese. We met only once
for coffee, but our conversation shaped the remainder of my
stay in Kyoto.

Earlier that summer, at a conference celebrating the bicen-
tennial of Henry David Thoreau's birth, I'd learned of a Japanese hermit who, like Thoreau, had withdrawn to a handmade
cabin in the woods and written about his experience. In the azure-
ceilinged Masonic hall in Concord, Massachusetts, an audience of
latter-day transcendentalists had listened as a Japanese scholar,
Yoshiko Ito, spoke of "the Thoreau of Japan" and showed us
slides of a thatch-roofed dwelling, a replica like that of Thoreau's
cabin by the parking lot at nearby Walden Pond. Despite my up-
coming trip, I hadn't thought to ask more questions then. Now I
did. Who was this hermit? Where was the replica of the hut—
might it be near enough to visit?

That's how I first heard—or *learned*—the name Kamo no
Chōmei and his book's title, *Hōjō-ki* (*The Ten Foot Square Hut*).
The book was a classic; all Japanese students read it. And Kamo
no Chōmei, a disgruntled nobleman of the Fujiwara court, had
renounced the world in Heian Kyoto, more than six hundred

years before Thoreau took to the woods of Concord. The replica of his hut could be found on the grounds of a Shinto shrine not far from our coffeehouse and the KU campus, on a promontory formed by the convergence of the Takano and Kamo Rivers, the latter providing the author's family name. *Hōjō-ki* had been "well translated" into English, my friend's former girlfriend told me, and I went back to the library—this time the mammoth modern one on North Campus, near the clock tower and camphor tree.

The book I came away with was slight—mercifully no *Walden*, with its ponderous opening chapter, "Economy." *Hōjō-ki* begins with a brief preamble, an invocation of the Buddhist doctrine of impermanence, setting the stage for Chōmei's choice to leave society and settle alone in the woods. Chōmei had been a court poet in the years before his retreat to a mountainside in exurban Hino, well to the south of Kyoto in Heian times. He would not, like Thoreau, give up his new way of life in little more than two years. The translators Yasuhiko Moriguchi and David Jenkins had rendered Chōmei's words in verse:

> *The flowing river*
> *never stops*
> *and yet the water*
> *never stays*
> *the same.*

> *Foam floats*
> *upon the pools,*
> *   scattering, re-forming,*
> *never lingering long.*

So it is with man
and all his dwelling places
here on earth.

Eventually I found three more English translations of *Hōjō-ki*, all in prose. I was glad to see that in two of them, the pesky "man/his" was translated inclusively: "So, too, it is with the people and dwellings of the world," in Anthony Chambers's rendition. But Chōmei had been a poet, and the line breaks and short stanzas of the Moriguchi-Jenkins version suited my diminished attention span. I used my visiting professor's library privileges to keep the slim volume close at hand in the coming months.

I liked the way Chōmei raised questions, delicately and with poignance, that his unknowing spiritual descendant Thoreau answered centuries later with vehemence:

And so the question,
where should we live?
And how?

Where to find
a place to rest a while?

And how bring
even short-lived peace
to our hearts?

Chōmei's *Hōjō-ki* really was poetry; Thoreau's *Walden*, with its justly famous second chapter, "Where I Lived and What I Lived For," was argument. When Thoreau retreated to Walden

Pond in July 1845, he had only recently discovered Buddhism, by way of a translation of the Lotus Sutra done by his transcendentalist colleague Elizabeth Peabody, working from the French of Eugène Burnouf, published in *The Dial* under his friend Ralph Waldo Emerson's editorship—the first English translation of any Buddhist text. Thoreau had to plead his case for the simple life, for solitude as boon and balm, to the unconverted Americans of a go-ahead era when cities glittered in the popular imagination.

Even if few practiced Buddhism as extremely as he or the other rustic ascetics of his time, Chōmei addressed knowing readers with the confidence he would be understood, his choice accepted, even lauded. He could cajole, enchant; he need not exhort. Without exciting curiosity or malicious gibes, he could make a remote cabin his home.

If your mind is not at peace
what use are riches?
The grandest hall
will never satisfy.

I love my lonely dwelling,
this one-room hut.

———

SCHOOL STARTED AND Yuri Nagira, the graduate student assigned as my guide, arrived. Yuri's specialty was Black American writers, her dissertation on the novels of Gloria Naylor. She knew little more than I did about Kamo no Chōmei and had never seen the replica of his hut. We took a taxi to the Shimogamo shrine, one of Kyoto's seventeen UNESCO World Heritage Sites, and wandered through its grounds, along a narrow brook shaded by towering broadleaf trees, some of them hundreds of years old. The trees impressed Yuri, a commuting student from Osaka, more than the shrine's formal gates and historic halls of worship. There were no trees like these in Osaka, she said. All had been burned or blasted in the war.

Yuri interpreted for me the curious scene at the entrance to the lesser Kawai shrine at Shimogamo's southernmost edge, where we'd been told to look for Chōmei's hut within a high-fenced enclosure housing an altar to the Shinto goddess Ta-mayorihime. Bevies of laughing teenaged girls were lined up to purchase what looked like Ping-Pong paddles, after which they clustered at tables supplied with plastic bins of colored pencils, sketching on the plywood ovals. Tamayorihime was said to be extraordinarily beautiful, Yuri explained. The girls were using the pencils to apply cosmetic colors to stylized features—eyes, mouth, cheeks—printed on one side of the paddles, cut in the shape of hand mirrors, then flipping them over to write wishes for beauty, both internal and external, on the back. I looked beyond the shrine's gates and saw that its interior walls were lined with racks holding these paddles, hundreds, maybe thousands of smiling made-up faces bearing their owners' hopes. No one besides Yuri and me had come to the Kawai shrine to honor Kamo no Chōmei, a man who had turned away from women and likely saw few faces, beautiful or otherwise, through his last eight years, 1208–1216, lived out on the Hino mountainside.

The replica, which, unlike Thoreau's parking-lot shack at

Walden, one could not enter, appeared a bit larger and of a more
ingenious design than the Concord hermit's. The dark wooden
structure, with walls made of four equal-sized panels anchored
with hinges to bamboo poles at each corner, was meant to be easily portable. Should Chōmei wish to relocate, all he need do was
cart the panels and poles to a new site, lay another foundation of
planks on the ground, attach the walls, and top them off with a
gently peaked roof. His hut, perhaps more tent than cabin, was a

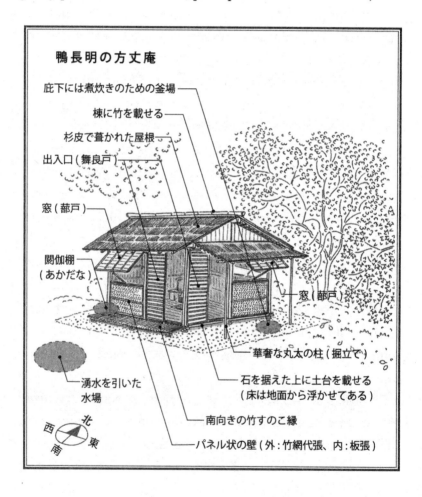

鴨長明の方丈庵

庇下には煮炊きのための釜場

棟に竹を載せる

杉皮で葺かれた屋根

出入口（舞良戸）

窓（蔀戸）

閼伽棚
（あかだな）

窓（蔀戸）

華奢な丸太の柱（掘立で）

湧水を引いた
水場

石を据えた上に土台を載せる
（床は地面から浮かせてある）

南向きの竹すのこ縁

パネル状の壁（外：竹網代張、内：板張）

北
西　東
南

harmonious square, filling most of the Kawai shrine's small interior courtyard.

The thatching I'd remembered from the slide lecture in Concord was not on the roof but comprised a low fence that appeared to be made of upended brushwood brooms, perhaps shielding the building from anticipated *Hōjō-ki* fans, or the potent vanity of female adolescents. Chōmei made no mention of a fence in his book, but he listed his home's contents, as Thoreau had his bed, desk, and famous three chairs—"one for solitude, two for friendship, three for society." Chōmei's bed was a heap of dried bracken on the floor. To his walls he affixed a shelf for musical instruments, another for sacred texts and musical scores, an altar for devotional offerings, an image of the Buddha shielded by a screen, a scroll bearing the words of the Lotus Sutra. Chōmei's quarters offered no provision for society or even friendship.

Perhaps it had been a mistake to situate the replica on the grounds of the bustling Shimogamo shrine, where Chōmei's father had once held high rank, a position the son expected to inherit but was denied for political reasons, contributing to his decision to leave the Heian court. This incongruous setting would have been like placing the replica of Thoreau's cabin alongside Concord's First Parish church, from which the transcendentalist had defiantly resigned as a young parishioner, or on busy Boston Common—or, considering the Kawai shrine's chief foot traffic, outside the Sephora shop on Newbury Street.

Yuri and I took photos of each other in front of the compact structure with our iPhones as young women streamed past us to deposit their mirror images on the racks. I knew I would return. And I did several days later, after discovering a frightening welt on my right ear that itched and burned and turned from red to bluish purple overnight. I paid eight hundred yen for a wooden paddle, sketched two delicate ears along with a ruby mouth and cobalt eyes, inscribed my wish—that the unsightly lump, the result, perhaps, of a spider bite received while I was sleeping on the futon in my ground-floor dwelling, would disappear—and placed my likeness on the rack nearest Kamo no Chōmei's ten-foot-square hut. One spirit or another would surely come to my assistance.

———

SCOTT'S VISIT IN October was another plan resulting from a calendrical misunderstanding on my part. I'd heard about Kyoto's spectacular autumns, the fall colors more striking even than those of the sugar maples, birches, and oaks I marveled over each year at home, and we scheduled Scott's trip to Japan accordingly. Fall is fall in the Northern Hemisphere, I'd assumed, only to learn that Kyoto's leaves turn much later than New England's, in a glorious red-and-orange revelation at mid-November. But we luxuriated in Kyoto's offseason, dining in top restaurants without reservations, checking into a rustic *ryokan* for one night on a whim, touring landmark temples and still-green gardens without waiting in line.

Although Scott had been hospitalized for a bout of congestive heart failure four years earlier, an aftereffect of chemotherapy for lymphoma nearly a decade before, it was my back injury we worried about—choosing chairs rather than tatami seating at meals, carrying little with us on our treks around the city. I didn't yet know that CHF does not come in bouts. It's an incurable condition, a gradual failing of the heart Scott accommodated to, taking pills to ease the burden on the weakening organ as it pumped vital fluids through his body and keeping the most dire facts of his case from me. The average CHF patient dies within five years of onset. Scott would make it to six.

We rode the subway and then a train to Kyoto's Fushimi Ward to take in one of the city's most popular sights: the Fushimi Inari shrine, reached by a winding uphill path passing beneath thousands of vermilion gates, the distinctive Shinto *torii*. As we approached the steepest section of trail, my back began to ache, Scott's breathing became labored, and we reversed direction, disappointed and hot. October was still summertime in Kyoto. Recovering in a teahouse near the train station, I studied my map and noticed that Hōkai-ji, the Buddhist temple at the base of Kamo no Chōmei's mountainside, was nearby, but we had no energy to venture farther.

On one of his last days in Japan, while I attended a graduate seminar, Scott took the *shinkansen* to Hiroshima, a private pilgrimage to the site of the devastated city his grandfather had viewed through binoculars as a forty-four-year-old chief pharmacist's mate from the deck of a U.S. Navy destroyer offshore in late summer 1945, inhaling the still-noxious air. The bomb saved the life of Professor Mizuno's uncle Susumu, but it cost Scott's grandfather his, along with the lives of so many hundreds of thousands at the time of the blast and after. Scott remembered his grandfather from childhood as a frail man confined to his bed, dying slowly of leukemia, gone at sixty-two, Scott's age on this visit.

"To understand / the world of today," Chōmei wrote in *Hōjō-ki*, "hold it up / to the world / of long ago." The poet had retreated from court life not only because of adverse political machinations—the "prelude to civil chaos," he wrote of the waning years of the Heian dynasty—but in a kind of despairing awe after witnessing a series of natural disasters that impressed upon him the truth of life's mutability. He cataloged them vividly—whirlwinds, floods, all-consuming fires—the last of which were often ignited by careless human hands and always exacerbated by the city's combustible man-made dwellings, both extravagant and humble. Chōmei's lines on the fiercest of these conflagrations could almost have served as an exhibition placard at the Hiroshima Peace Memorial Museum:

> *The wind blew wildly—*
> *this way! that way!—*
> *and the fire spread,*
> *like an unfolding fan.* . . .

> *Some suffocated by smoke*
> *fell upon the ground.*
> *Some swallowed by flames*
> *died at once.*

> *Some scarce able*
> *to save themselves,*
> *lost all their worldly goods.*

> *Many treasures*
> *reduced to ash!*

> *Dreadful,*
> *dreadful loss!*

THERE HAD BEEN no more North Korean missile flyovers since mid-September, but in early November, the third and most intense of that autumn's typhoons struck Kyoto, uprooting a venerable pine on South Campus, the shaggy cousin to the manicured camphor by the North Campus clock tower. The hundred-foot pine had dominated a courtyard near the squatters' dorms, and when I passed by on the way to my office I often found signs advertising concerts or dance parties hand-painted on large plywood panels leaning against the tree's broad base. The typhoon's winds blew through late on a Saturday night, but mercifully the pine went down when no one was around, crushing the corner of a shelter for the bike racks that were now nearly always crammed, but otherwise doing no harm.

The toppled pine lay in state for several days, the immense bulb of earth encasing its roots, now shockingly exposed to light and air, adding another ten feet to its length. Students gathered in small clusters, hugging each other and crying, or simply standing in silence, paying respect. Then the grounds crew arrived with chain saws to slice the massive trunk and limbs, some as large as individual trees, into sections and cart them away. I plucked a pine cone from one of the boughs, planning to bring it home as a souvenir of my days at KU, which were dwindling in number, and placed it on a paper plate left from a grad student gathering on the conference table in my office. A week later I arrived to find its scales had exploded across the tabletop. The temperature outdoors had dropped at last, and the building's heat had come on, drying my memento mori, which proceeded to declare its living purpose: the dispersion of seeds.

The typhoon had also taken down many of the towering stalks in the world-famous bamboo grove in Arashiyama, a section of Kyoto too far to the west for me to reach on foot. A new friend, Masako Takeda, Japan's foremost Emily Dickinson scholar, took me there by a series of bus and train connections to tour a half dozen temples and their gardens. The leaves were beginning to turn and the crowds were picking up, but Masako, nearly as shy as the poet whose works she translated, knew how to evade them. We arrived at Tenryu-ji, another World Heritage Site, just as the gates opened on a Sunday, rapidly paced its paths and hallways, stopped to admire the celebrated reflecting pond, took our vegan lunch before we were hungry, then exited to the bamboo grove in noon shade rather than wait, as the tourists surely would, for the sun to sink and irradiate the enormous fronds, providing the classic view.

Masako led me, instead, down a deserted country lane, past open fields, to Rakushisha, the "Hut of Fallen Persimmons," home of the seventeenth-century poet Mukai Kyorai, a disciple of the haiku master Bashō. This small house, twice the size of Chōmei's hut, with a series of interlocking rooms and a densely thatched roof straight out of a Bruegel landscape, was also a replica. But it had been constructed by one of Kyorai's own students centuries ago, and the persimmon tree we sat beneath in a well-kept garden was said to be the same from which Bashō, on his three known visits to his pupil, had partaken of fruit. The glistening orbs hung heavy above us. November's glory had arrived.

It was not hard to persuade Masako to guide me to Hōkai-ji temple in Fushimi Ward on a balmy day in late November, in search of the original site of Kamo no Chōmei's hut. Unlike Professor Mizuno and his graduate students, all of them smitten early with a passion for American literature, Masako had begun her academic career as a student of Japanese aesthetic culture. Required by law to retire from teaching at sixty-five, she was newly released into a life of leisure, and had added master classes in tea ceremony and the art of mixing scents to her scholarly work and the seminars on Dickinson she offered to neighbors at her home in Osaka. She had time for the trip to Hino, and she shared my curiosity.

Another series of train rides brought us to a hilly suburb, eerily vacant in this season of high tourism. On a recent evening I'd stood in line for over an hour in the icy darkness with Yuri, my grad student guide, and her thirteen-year-old daughter, waiting to enter the grounds of Eikando and walk its crowded paths to witness a "light-up"—the temple's allées of red-and-orange maples all aglow, underlit by the artificial fire of electric lamps. Now Masako and I were the only visitors to Hōkai-ji as the midafternoon sun began to drop behind the western mountains of Arashiyama, its slanted rays illuminating the yellow-leaved shrubbery lining the walkways and casting into shadow the temple's small cluster of wooden buildings. We peeked into one and gaped at a wall covered with what appeared to be a multitude of infants' bibs, mildewing in the dank air. At the unmanned information booth we found a laminated fact sheet explaining that Hōkai-ji's guardian spirits were thought to aid nursing mothers. Supplicants could purchase bibs and pin them to the wall, helping to support the temple's upkeep while making visible their prayers for easy, bountiful lactation.

Masako phoned the number written on the fact sheet and summoned the temple's presiding monk, dressed in work clothes and high rubber boots, who nodded at her inquiries about Chōmei's reclusion. He directed us to the first in a series of signposts that led us up the mountainside, past stucco town houses that gave way to terraced fields, a fenced-in community tennis court, and, finally, a dusty lot at the base of a heavily wooded ravine. At the far end a sort of outdoor umbrella stand stocked with slender tree limbs—homemade walking sticks offered to Chōmei's pilgrims by a local senior citizens' hiking club—marked the trailhead, the start of a narrow path that inclined steeply upward, overhung by trees still bearing green-and-yellow leaves.

During my months in Kyoto, I'd grown accustomed to the city's meticulously landscaped gardens, domesticated Edens that showed off individual trees or symmetrically planted groves to best advantage, allowing them space to expand and visitors room to admire. Here was raw nature, trees growing so close upon one another they were nearly indistinguishable. Vines in high branches connected their hosts in a muddled biota whose population I could not begin to name or number. Chōmei had called these "spindle trees." As we ascended, the stream Chōmei relied on for water grew ever more distant in the crook of the ravine below. Trees pressed in, narrowing the trail, and we walked single file. Sunlight filtered down the ravine, reminding us it was day, but our path lay in what must have been perpetual shadow, and the temperature fell.

At last we reached a ledge marked by an engraved granite slab and a ceramic vase with a bouquet of fresh roses left by a previous visitor. Nature crowded and almost choked us here, but Chōmei had somehow cleared this scarcely level patch of earth, settled his movable hut upon it, and achieved the solitude he sought. "The valley is thick with trees," he wrote in *Hōjō-ki*, "but I have a view / of the Western heavens, / focus for meditation."

On his rough mountainside, Chōmei did not forget human-kind or the devastations he'd witnessed. Indeed, he devoted some of his time to writing about them. But here there was little distinction between life within and life without. The rhythms of nature replaced those of court life and offered psychic shelter from remembered cataclysm.

Each season had its character. In winter, the snow settled "like human sin" only to melt "in atonement." Spring brought wisteria, blooming "like a holy purple cloud"; summer, the chattering cuckoos.

In autumn
the voices of evening cicadas
fill the ear.

They seem to grieve
this husk of a world.

———

ON THANKSGIVING I took a leisurely *kaiseki* lunch at a favorite restaurant with Keiko Beppu, a retired professor of modern poetry who, in the 1990s, had become one of Japan's first female college presidents and the first woman president of the American Literature Society of Japan. She explained her impressive career, telling me that as a young woman her husband had divorced her when she'd been unable to bear children. The rejection had inspired in her a fierce desire to make something of her life; aside from her notable presidencies and long list of publications, she was the beloved mentor to many of the female scholars I met during my stay.

That evening, I received an email from Scott: a bad cold had kept him away from our family Thanksgiving dinner. He was coughing too much to phone, but he was sure he'd be well again soon. It was just a cold. Our landlady sent word too. Scott's cough alarmed her. When was I coming home?

In a matter of days I would fly to Boston. I had found Kamo no Chōmei's place of retreat. And I'd reached the end of Nathaniel Hawthorne's fourth novel, *The Marble Faun*, a "romance" of three expatriate artists in Rome, culminating in a tragic death. Hawthorne had written the novel during his own residence in Italy, a country whose opulent palazzi, lush gardens, and gilded sanctuaries must have enthralled an untraveled American of the 1850s as Japan bewitched me now. Hawthorne would never complete another book, although he didn't know it then. "This sunny, shadowy, breezy, wandering life," his narrator muses, in which the artist "seeks for beauty as his treasure, and gathers for his winter's honey what is but a passing fragrance to all other men, is worth living for, come afterwards what may."

———

DURING THE SEVENTEEN months of Scott's dying, of which there were several when we could still pretend this was not the end, I added poems to my memorized store: Marianne Moore's "What Are Years?"—"He / sees deep and is glad, who / accedes to mortality." Dylan Thomas's "The force that through the green fuse drives the flower." Finally, Robert Lowell's "Obit"—"After loving you so much, can I forget / you for eternity, and have no other choice?"

When Scott was gone, my days were filled first with the business of his death, then with lunches, dinners, concerts, and movies with friends; precious afternoons and evenings with my daughters, their spouses and children. It was only when COVID-19 arrived, depriving me of those cherished comforts as the anniversary of Scott's death approached—even the probate court closed down—that my daily solitary pacing in my neighborhood brought me back to Kyoto and *Hōjō-ki*.

I had not remembered that after the whirlwinds, floods, and fires—

> *. . . on top of all*
> *a great plague broke out,*
>   *stood the world upon its head.*

In Kyoto, forty thousand died in two months' time. The food supply to the city was cut off, bringing famine and, with it, "so many other sights / to break the heart." Bodies lay in the streets; babies cried, attempting to suckle at their dead mothers' breasts. Chōmei observed of "Loving couples"—

> *the one whose love was deeper*
> *always died first.*

> *They held back,*
>   *gave the meager food*
>   *to their dearest.*

I was not sick or hungry, but I lost friends to the virus; others contracted the illness and were slow to recover. I could not see my daughters. As my thinking became disordered in the shocking blur of hours, days, and weeks, I asked myself: Was I still here because Scott had loved me most? Our circumstances were not the same as those of Chōmei's starving lovers, but Scott had selflessly given me a kind of food: a period of solitude in which to learn how to feed myself, although my time in Japan left him alone for three of his last twenty months in the world.

"I'm not worried about you," Scott told me one day over a dinner stalled by his vanished appetite. Desperate with worry for *him*, and foolishly proud of managing our lives and his care, I hadn't known what he meant or why he said it. But I had that now as well, his belief in me, *come what may*. And yes, maybe his excess love: the surplus I would need to live on without him, until I, too, fronted the truth of life's mutability—

> *Great houses fade away,*
> *to be replaced by lesser ones.*

> *Thus too those*
> *who live in them. . . .*

> *They are born into dusk*
> *and die as the day dawns,*
> *like that foam*
> *upon the water.*

LEFT-HANDED

CHRISTMAS WOULDN'T BE CHRISTMAS WITHOUT an exchange of gifts among my two grandmothers, mother, and aunt featuring the trait they shared: all four were left-handed. Waiting for them under the tree might be left-handed oven mitts or can openers, kitchen gadgets too mundane to pass as gifts for righties, but treasures to the matriarchal quartet. I'll never forget the crows of delight one Christmas morning as they unwrapped identical packages to find pairs of left-handed sewing scissors, the first designed and widely marketed not just with upside-down handles but with inverted blades to make cutting fabric easy.

All four of them sewed—my mother and her sister-in-law, my left-handed aunt, to economize on dresses for themselves and their daughters, six between them. My maternal grandmother specialized in holiday-themed projects: red corduroy vests for the men of the family, embroidered table runners. My father's mother had never taken to the sewing machine and instead knitted afghans and scarves. Left-handedness may have been the reason she never progressed beyond the basic garter stitch. Left-handed knitters, I would later learn, are sometimes forced to study themselves in the mirror to master more complicated stitches pictured in instruction manuals issued for the right-handed 90 percent. But when I was young in the 1950s, when the home was woman's domain, left-handedness meant the omnipotence of motherhood. Surely I would grow up to be a left-handed woman too.

Slowly I began to realize that would never be. My right hand took over when I scribbled with crayons and when I learned to print letters in pencil at school. I had a new best friend who was left-handed—new because I'd been skipped into second grade in the middle of my first grade year. I read too well and had to leave my old friends behind. Catherine lived up the street, and she was an ace at jacks. With one hand—her left—she bounced one of her father's old golf balls on the cool concrete of the shaded front porch where we sat cross-legged facing each other, and swiftly scooped up the scuffed six-pointed stars in the same hand, first one per bounce, then in twos and threes, on up to the full set of ten, just in time to catch the ball as it fell. I was mesmerized. She'd won before I could even take a turn.

On a Friday in April that first and second grade year, my mother's parents arrived from San Francisco to stay with us for spring vacation. Instead of walking home from school with Catherine, I spotted my grandparents' red-and-white Plymouth waiting for me on the street beyond the chain-link fence that bordered the asphalt playground and ran to meet them. I ran with my red plaid lunch box in my left hand and white sweater dangling from my right to wind between my legs and trip me; I fell flat, arms outstretched, my forehead landing on the metal clasp that held the lunch box shut. Even at age six I knew to press my white sweater against the bleeding gash. My grandmother scooped me up, and soon I was in a doctor's office, facing a needle threaded with coarse black floss in a man's right hand.

To this day, if I look closely at my left eyebrow in the mirror, I can see the scar that marks me on the left side: as a woman like my mother, like *her* mother, to whom I'd run with a heart full of love and need.

———

NO ONE TOLD me, but I knew why my grandparents had come to stay through the school holiday. My father had lost his job again, the one for which we'd moved away from the grandmother we knew so well that my older brother, younger sister, and I had called her "Plain Grandma" to distinguish her from my father's Wellesley-educated mother in Altadena, the librarian we'd dubbed "Lady Grandma" from the distance of our old home in Los Altos. Now Plain Grandma was "Granny," and Lady Grandma, simply "Grandma," as she became more familiar to us; through the past summer I'd seen Grandma every Saturday morning for the story hour she led in the children's room, and then I'd spent Thursdays after school reading my way through the shelves under her watchful eye while my mother taught children's classes at the nearby Pasadena Art Museum (later the Norton Simon Museum). But now my mother was working every day as a secretary at our church. My sister and I wore our house keys on long white shoelaces tied around our necks and tucked under our blouses; my brother had pockets in the jeans only boys were allowed to wear to school.

That week, as my eyebrow healed, I loved lying on the double bed in my parents' bedroom to watch Granny work her way through the pile of my father's freshly washed dress shirts that filled the bentwood rocker where, she said, my mother had nursed me as an infant and Granny had nursed my mother. She sprinkled each shirt with water from a blue glass bottle topped with a metal cap full of tiny holes like a salt shaker's, and rolled the damp fabric into a ball to moisten thoroughly; then she unfurled the white or pale blue oxford cloth shirts one by one and methodically pressed the hot iron to smooth the collar, yoke, arms, and back and front panels on the ironing board that was a permanent fixture in the room. Like my mother, Granny wielded the electric iron expertly with her left hand, although she mistrusted its steam setting. Years later, when I did my own ironing, I'd have to switch the cord from one side of the board to the other before starting in, to avoid entangling the fabric as I ran the hot appliance over the flowered shifts and A-line skirts in solid colors I'd sewn at our Singer.

As she ironed, Granny sang songs she'd learned from her voice-teacher mother, a single mom left by her husband to raise their two daughters in Oakland through the first two decades of the century. Her parents' divorce was a source of shame to my grandmother; she never spoke of it. She told me instead about her own first grade year, when the teacher forbade her to write with her left hand and finally, in exasperation, bound Granny's left arm to her chest so she wouldn't be tempted. Was she also the only child in the class without a father at home? After my grandparents drove back north that spring, I looked closely at the handwriting on the envelopes that arrived every week addressed to my mother (long-distance calls were too expensive) and ad-

mired the even right-slanting loops, knowing the price in humili-
ation and effort my grandmother had paid to achieve them.

My mother's name on those envelopes was Elva Marshall,
but when I looked for samples of her handwriting beyond the
grocery lists she dashed off in the morning before leaving for
work, left hand raised slightly above the notepad to avoid inking
the side of her hand, I found her signature in the bottom right
corners of the watercolor landscapes she'd painted as an art major in college, which hung in many of the rooms in our house:
Elva Spiess. The unfamiliar name she'd shared with her parents
appeared in upright, spidery black—the same ink as the fine lines
that made sense of otherwise blurry strokes of color suggesting mountains, lakes, pines. There were a few paintings marked
with tiny lowercase initials, "esm," as if the letters formed one
word—here were the yellows and browns of the mustard fields
and rolling hills we sometimes drove past near our old house in
Los Altos. I knew she'd won a blue ribbon in a community art
show shortly before we'd moved away. But I couldn't picture
my mother with a paintbrush in her hand.

She just didn't have the time. A wooden door propped on file
cabinets served as her worktable running along one wall of the
bedroom, opposite the ironing board. When I had trouble sleeping at night, I found her there, working under lamplight, gouging
inscrutable designs in blocks of wood eventually to yield black-
and-white prints—stark representations of scenes like those in
her paintings I'd see when, after long intervals, she'd carefully
peel a sheet of rice paper from the sticky inked finished carving—
schooling herself in patience as she mastered a new medium, chosen because it allowed for interruption. She was sleepy, and so was
I. Still, she tolerated my appearance at her elbow, my confession

of worries or a nightmare. Far more disruptive, I knew, were her day jobs, which shifted over the years, and, I could only guess, the anxiety she held at bay about my father's mental illness. Many nights, and often in the afternoon when my siblings and I returned from school, he slept with a book open on his lap in the padded armchair downstairs in our former playroom, which served as his office for the consulting business he'd established only to rapidly fail.

Skilled as she was with her left hand, my mother frequently apologized for a clumsiness she believed her dominant left side brought upon her. She'd never learned to ride a bike and swam only a tentative side stroke, head out of the water. At dinner parties, she asked to be seated at a left corner so she wouldn't bump elbows with a right-handed neighbor, and I never saw her gesticulate with either hand, certainly not her left, which often rested in her lap or dangled limp beside her when she stood in company. She wore her thick blond hair parted on the right, as if to compensate, but for years she set my own part on the left as I sat on a stool in the backyard, white bedsheet clothespinned around my neck, submitting to her best efforts with a right-handed pair of haircutting scissors. We looked alike, people said—blue eyes, bobbed hair—except for this.

As the '60s came on, I stopped letting my mother cut my hair and grew it long, as did my sister and most of our girl cousins, all of us right-handed. With our hair parted in the middle, our faces open to the future, we'd have a better time of it: embark on careers, make egalitarian matches, if we married at all. In the California of well-funded public schools and libraries, scenic state parks and beaches, we had read and swum and biked and, yes, still sewn our way toward womanhood, and we would not be sidelined. The year I turned eighteen, the year of the left-handed scissors, 1972—when Fiskars took its innovative red-handled design worldwide—was the last Christmas I spent with my family. I was done with left-handed women.

———

SOME OF THE statistics on left-handers surprised me when I finally took the time to look them up. Men, for example, constitute a small but significant majority of southpaws. One controversial finding states that left-handed people of both sexes die younger than righties; indeed, counter to the expected outcome among heterosexual couples, my mother and *her* mother and my left-handed aunt were all survived by their somewhat older right-handed male spouses— by seventeen, seven, and four years. When, a half century after that last Christmas at home, I compared the ages at death of my four left-handed female forebears and their spouses, including my paternal grandmother who died in 1986 at ninety-three, nine years older than her husband at his death, I found an average disadvantage of over six years for the left-handed women. That's even higher than the nearly five years reported by the psychologist Stanley Coren in *The Left-Hander Syndrome: The Causes and Consequences of Left-Handedness*. Mine is a small and idiosyncratic sample, not enough to defend Coren's thesis against the rebuttals of subsequent researchers, like Rik Smits, who debunked the "myth of high left-handed mortality" in *The Puzzle of Left-Handedness*. Still, no writer on left-handedness disputes the long history of prejudice that may contribute to a shortened life span, as Coren argues, starting with the Anglo-Saxon root word for "left"— *lyft*—which means "weak" or "broken."

Other writers dwell on the Latinate "sinistral," an adjective meaning "left-handed," which shares its root with "sinister," a derivation all the more dispiriting to the left-hander, who must become inured to the myriad denotations and connotations of "right"—practically all of them positive, unless you're a political leftist. One never studies to get a "left" answer on a test or hopes to be found "in the left"—even as one might be left out, left behind, or make a solitary dinner of leftovers. An idea that comes out of left field is unexpected, if not unwelcome, and a left-handed compliment can hurt.

The Latinate adjective "dextral" describes a right-hander: dexterous. Lefties who study the French language soon learn that their handedness is *gauche,* socially awkward and clumsy in English as well as in French. According to Coren, left-handers really are accident-prone: 20 percent more likely to have an accidental injury when playing sports, 25 percent more likely at work, 49 percent more likely at home, and "51 percent more likely to have an accident-related injury when using a tool, machine, or other implement." Living left-handed in a right-handed world incurs risk; right-handedness is protective, a rarely examined source of privilege. Little wonder that in times past, and in parts of the world still today, parents and teachers resorted to extreme measures in discouraging young children from using their left hands at school or even in play. A friend my own age recalls her mother swatting down her left hand when, as a toddler, she reached with it instinctively to pick up her toys; she became a righty, though if you toss a tennis ball in her direction, she'll catch it with her left hand. My grandmother never told me by what means her teacher bound her left hand to her chest, but I've read about a leather belt with buckles specifically designed to strap the left arm behind the student's back, used in Victorian-era classrooms when a child failed to keep her left hand in check by sitting on it, as ordered.

Not many paid attention, it seems, to a lengthy treatise in defense of left-handers published in 1891, over a decade before my grandmother entered school: *The Right Hand: Left-Handedness*. The author, Sir David Wilson, a scholar of prehistory (a term he coined) and president of the University of Toronto, aimed to prove "the folly of persistently striving to suppress an innate faculty of exceptional aptitude." Wilson marshaled archaeological, anthropological, and linguistic evidence, along with the latest theories of brain science, to champion "the dishonored hand." At the time, it was believed that left-handers made up only about 2 percent of the population, and much of Wilson's research was directed toward establishing left-handedness as a naturally occurring phenomenon through the ages. There have always been left-handers—why not let them alone? By 1920, the figure rose to 4 percent, as the practice of "retraining" left-handers to use their right hands began to fade from classrooms along with other physical means of regulating student behavior. By midcentury, 10 percent was the accepted figure, and it has stuck. Manufacturers in the post–World War II commercial boom started to introduce goods that catered to what now seemed a significant market. The Danish architect Arne Jacobsen's famous off-kilter stainless steel soupspoon, its bowl set nearer to the lips than its handle, was produced by Georg Jensen in both left- and right-handed models from the time of its initial casting in 1957. The household implements my female elders exchanged as gifts at Christmastime filled the novelty shelves of kitchenware aisles in department stores.

The 1970s brought not just Fiskars's lefty sewing shears but a honeymoon with left-handedness, as books and news articles on neuroscience introduced readers to the concept of the brain's differently functioning hemispheres. Studies of the brain-injured had long since established that motor functions, including handedness, were controlled by the opposite brain hemisphere—left-handers by the right brain, right-handers by the left. As researchers, aided by new technology permitting brain scans of healthy subjects, began to locate other functions, such as language and sensory perception, in distinct portions of the brain, a dualism took hold in the popular imagination: "The left brain speaks, the right brain laughs," to borrow the formulation of the science journalist Ransom Stephens. The right brain was believed to be the locus of creativity. Left-handers, less dominated by the "inner accountant" residing in their left brains, must be more imaginative—a quality increasingly valued not just in the arts but also by venture capitalists in the burgeoning tech sector. Famous left-handers were cited as confirmation: Leonardo, Michelangelo, Einstein, Picasso. Betty Edwards's enduringly popular *Drawing on the Right Side of the Brain*, first published in 1979, capitalized on the dichotomy, promising to teach the right-handed majority how to access powers lying dormant within their weaker right brains.

I'm not sure whether my mother benefited from the pro-lefty mood in her last decade of life. More likely the fact that she finally ended her marriage to my troubled father in 1977—the same year all three of her children, thanks to varying degrees of waywardness, graduated from college—accounted for her return to art making in her sixties, this time with etching plates and a hand-operated press, another new medium. In any case, the valorization of left-handedness turned out to be short-lived. During the years after my mother's death in 1991, close inspection of archival photographs would reveal that both Einstein and Picasso had been misidentified as lefties; improved scanning technology exposed the right brain–left brain dichotomy as mostly false. More sophisticated imaging captured frequent instances of collaboration between the sides of the brain as well as substantial variation among individuals. Studies of left-handers found that only a minority are fully right-hemisphere dominant. Many right-handers are, unexpectedly, right-brain dominant.

Uncertainty also reigns when it comes to determining the origins of left-handedness. What makes a person left-handed? Is it a matter of "habit" or "preference," terms that many studies of the subject still employ? And if not—if handedness is innate, its source in our genes—why were none of the eight children of left-handed mothers and grandmothers in my generation left-handed?

There is simply no good answer—or no single answer. A large-scale population study by Carolien de Kovel, Amaia Carrión-Castillo, and Clyde Francks published in *Scientific Reports* in 2019 found that "left-handedness was very weakly heritable" and might as easily be affected by "birthweight, being part of a multiple birth, season of birth, breastfeeding, and sex," along with "the year and location of birth, likely due to cultural effects," such as societal enforcement of retraining. "Preferring one hand over the other," wrote Linda Searing of *The Washington Post* that same year, "could be simply random variation." Nevertheless, due in part to recent studies that have uncovered a link between left-handedness and neurodiversity (in one instance, 28 percent of people on the autism spectrum were found to be left-handed, compared with 10 percent in the general population), sperm banks now provide clients with information on donors' handedness. The designer baby would, presumably, grow up right-handed.

I WASN'T LEFT-HANDED, but from the day I first pulled on my socks and shoes and tied them by myself, I started with my left foot before my right. Perhaps at first I was copying my mother, but soon it became a conscious choice to give precedence, in this at least, to my weaker left side. I was a strong righty—good (for a girl, kids said) at throwing a softball the distance to home from the outfield, a reliable hitter when I was up at bat, batting right-handed. In kickball, my right foot sent the red rubber ball flying well past the infield, and I was deft at four square with my right hand, especially during the few weeks in fifth grade after I fell down roller-skating and wore a cast on my right wrist, adding force to each right-armed smack of the ball into my opponents' squares.

But sometimes at home, before I went out to face the world right-handed, it felt like too much. Left was where life started, with my left-handed mother; where sentences began when I read a book or wrote, from left to right. Maybe, too, I was uncomfortable, as a girl, with the force I was capable of exerting with my right hand, arm, or leg. There were no sports teams to play on, just the pickup games in our neighborhood and improvised matches on the playground at recess. What good would my strength do me? It won me no friends, among either boys or girls.

I left this behind, too, when I traveled east for college and stayed. I believed I'd escaped Southern California's surf's-up sexism and, all the more oppressive for the guilt I felt in abandoning her, the weight of my mother's disappointment as an artist—the paintings never painted—and in her marriage. But when I began to write, I found myself attracted to almosts, to might-have-beens, to compromise—so often woman's story. My first book was a set of case studies based on interviews with single women in their thirties, a half generation ahead of me as I worked on the book in my late twenties. These were women like the older students I'd envied for their self-possession as they smoked Gauloises and discussed French feminist theory while writing their senior theses when I was a freshman at Bennington College; who'd founded women's centers and rape crisis centers and taught self-defense classes in Cambridge and Berkeley, where I'd worked as a secretary when I dropped out of college for two years; who told their abortion stories at pro-choice rallies and later organized Take Back the Night marches; who applied to law, medical, and business schools and took seats among classes of mostly men.

But by the early 1980s, the Equal Rights Amendment had failed. Ronald Reagan was president. Faith in movement politics waned, and these same women were taking stock, many of them disappointed in an entirely different way from my mother: overworked and overlooked in professions where they'd pioneered, lonely and wanting children they worried they might never bear. They were lonely, too, in an existential way; their drive to upend the status quo rested on a belief that they were *firsts*, no women had traveled this road before. The book was published in 1984, the Orwellian year that had once seemed so impossibly far off.

A few years later I was startled to find my book singled out in the opening pages of Susan Faludi's *Backlash* as representative of an alarming new critique of women's progress, undermining the values of feminism. That had not been my aim. I'd simply been reporting on what I heard: a complexity that drew me, inexorably, to biography—whole lives. With my next book, I planned to test the truth of my thirtysomething subjects' sense of their historical uniqueness. Couldn't we find company and even inspiration in the past?

I wasn't alone in this project, and I wasn't first. I had excellent models: Nancy Milford's full-scale biography *Zelda*, about F. Scott Fitzgerald's talented and troubled wife; Jean Strouse's *Alice James*, on the brilliant and not-quite-forgotten younger sister of novelist Henry and philosopher William, a lifelong invalid; Phyllis Rose's *Parallel Lives: Five Victorian Marriages*, in which only one woman in the quintet of writers' pairings, George Eliot, prevailed against matrimony to achieve lasting fame. I settled on the Peabody sisters as my subjects: three women of America's nineteenth-century cultural renaissance whose proximity to famous men, either as wives or friends, had ensured that their letters and journals were preserved and archived, providing me with access to their inner lives. As I researched and wrote, biographies of James Joyce's wife, Nora; Robert Lowell's first wife, Jean Stafford; and Vladimir Nabokov's adored Véra, by Brenda Maddox, Ann Hulbert, and Stacy Schiff, appeared as beacons on my path.

These same years brought plenty of biographies of indisputably heroic "foremothers": Nell Irvin Painter on Sojourner Truth, Susan Quinn on Marie Curie, Deirdre Bair on Simone de Beauvoir and Anaïs Nin, Susan Ware on Amelia Earhart, Kay Mills on Fannie Lou Hamer, Judith Thurman on Isak Dinesen and Colette, Hermione Lee on Virginia Woolf. Writing from a feminist perspective, these biographers didn't simply celebrate the already well-known; they wrote openly of the contradictory and sometimes scanty historical record, and refused to dodge controversy, in order to achieve the fullest possible portraits of complicated, often conflicted women.

But triumph over the odds didn't interest me then. The odds did. What measure of opposition—from culture, community, family—could a bright, ambitious woman tolerate? What way forward would she find and take? I'd married at twenty-six, and within a decade I'd assumed primary responsibility for raising the two daughters my husband and I named Sara and Josephine—for ancestors, but also after the heroines of my favorite children's books, *A Little Princess* and *Little Women,* clever, bookish girls of long ago whose innermost thoughts supplied much of their stories' drama. The outcomes weren't the point; in fact, in the case of Jo March, the conclusion was hard to take. Back in the Pasadena bedroom I'd shared with my sister, I'd read the two books over and over to commune with sympathetic spirits, girls who struggled to find their way. As I researched and wrote my own book, I was still struggling, uncertain how to get "my" work done while also doing the always more urgent work of the household. The book took twenty years to finish—virtually the whole of my daughters' childhoods—a period during which the Peabody sisters' intellectual and creative presence kept me company. I was home with my daughters every day after school, counting myself lucky, unlike my mother, to be there.

After *The Peabody Sisters* was published, readers often asked if I had a favorite among the three. I insisted I didn't, but I'd learned an important lesson from the youngest, Sophia, a talented artist who never quite seemed to get down to work. Always careful to maintain a historian's dispassionate perspective on my subjects as I wrote, I nonetheless allowed myself privately to compare Sophia's slim output of oil paintings, the last completed during the year before her first child was born, with my mother's early watercolors, which had shown such promise. I began to fear for my own future. Was I going the same route—might I never finish this book?

Sophia Peabody was barred, as a woman, from study in the few art academies in America, and propriety prevented her from painting models in the nude, critical to mastering principles of anatomy. She learned to paint by copying the work of her well-known male mentors. Her copies sold for substantial prices, but she often felt tormented: she would "never be satisfied till I *create* something." Family members, friends, and teachers all expected great things of her, but Sophia couldn't acquire the skills she needed to succeed, and she knew it. When the pain of thwarted ambition and disappointing others' hopes became overwhelming, she retreated into illness. Or perhaps it was the other way around: psychic pain brought on illness that impeded her work. This was Sophia's inward drama, which she resolved by learning to tolerate the conflict and schooling herself to accept the possibility that she might never "create." She refused to let others judge her, or to judge herself, by outward accomplishment. "I create—not with hands," but "within," she wrote in her journal, describing the pleasure she took in visualizing a gallery of works she might never paint but that nonetheless could fill her ample imagination.

I came to accept that I might never complete my book, that I might have attempted something too difficult for me, a project made impossible by the constraints on my writing hours. I had chosen in favor of the living people I most cared about. I would not let myself believe I was a failure if I didn't finish. Then, at long last, the book was done.

————

I'M SEATED AT a broad oak table in the high-ceilinged reading room of Radcliffe's Schlesinger Library on the History of Women in America, where in years past I've pored over gossipy diary entries from the Peabody sisters' stay in a Boston boardinghouse in the 1830s and Elizabeth Bishop's comradely letters and postcards to Adrienne Rich from the 1970s. Today in the room with me there are scholars studying the manuscripts of Betty Friedan and June Jordan; on other days researchers might come to examine the papers of Susan B. Anthony, Helen Keller, Angela Davis, Julia Child, Judy Chicago, or Ruth Handler, the inventor of Barbie. I'm here to read the letters and diaries of my mother and grandmothers. The Schlesinger Library values the papers of ordinary women too. In the end, my left-handed women had followed me to the East Coast.

I'd skimmed through the packets of letters folded into stamped envelopes, the hastily scrawled postcards, the jotted-in datebooks and clothbound journals, when they reached me in several cardboard boxes at home in the Boston suburbs after my mother's death in 1991 at sixty-eight, a year younger than I am now. My second daughter was just a year old. I had so much else to do, and the letters drew me back into a past I'd wanted to leave behind. I stowed them away on the floor of a closet already stuffed with spare sheets and towels for a family of four. And then fifteen years later, divorce uprooted us all; my family-first ethic hadn't withstood the frightening episodes of depression and hypomania that, eerily for me as the daughter of a man diagnosed during my childhood with manic depression, took hold of my husband at midlife. Once again, in a hastily planned move, I had neither the time nor the will to sort through the letters. The Schlesinger took them in 2008.

Am I ready now? I start with Granny's love letters, written during a year of forced separation after her wedding in February 1918, when my grandfather had enlisted in the navy and shipped out on a submarine chaser headed for Europe. She was twenty; he was twenty-three. Her right-slanting loops are carefully formed, the work of a recent high school graduate, and written in a fountain pen's dark ink rather than blue ballpoint, but still instantly recognizable to me. There's passion in these pages addressed to "Dearest" and "lover" and "Man of Mine," filled with jaunty accounts of her days as a bookkeeper's assistant and evenings in rehearsal for church theatricals, meant to buoy her young husband's spirits: ample evidence of the beginnings of a lifelong romance that would be secured by my grandfather's safe return from the war in January 1919.

Then suddenly—shockingly, to me—in a letter from September 1918, Granny is confiding what she never told me on those faraway afternoons in my parents' bedroom. She writes that she hopes they will have sons—"Do you know one reason why I want them boys Dear? So you won't have any other woman near you." And: "Did I ever tell you that when I was born, my father didn't look at me for days?" He'd wanted a son; his second-born daughter was one girl too many. After that, "how miserable he made Mama." Her father moved out, sought "other" women. She saw him rarely as she grew up, always to be reminded that he wished she and her older sister were boys. Only when her father was dying, the year before she met my grandfather, did he welcome his two grown daughters into his home. "He asked me to kiss him the last time we went and outside I wiped my lips off on Mama's cheeks"— transferring her father's unwanted kiss to her mother, who still mourned her lost love.

At my worktable in the Schlesinger I go on to read through dozens more file folders of chronologically arranged sheets of paper— my father's courtship letters, the weekly missives exchanged by my mother and grandmother spanning half a century—which, though filled with fresh detail, merely confirm a story I already know and, to a large extent, had witnessed myself: the wreck of my mother's hopes for a happy marriage and career as a painter. It's the surprising, swift narrative of a dual rejection—my grandmother for being a girl, her mother for giving birth to girls—that stays with me as the revelation of a primal injury to the women of my family, so very personal in its immediate effects, yet essentially impersonal, arbitrary, a random variation, like being left-handed. Womanhood as stigma. This is an old story, too, threaded through billions of lives across centuries and around the globe.

I turn back to the September 1918 letter and find, beyond the riveting tale, words I'd lost on my first shocked reading, but nearly as startling. "I never wished I was a boy though," Granny asserts. Could I have been so unwavering? "A boy can never be as close to his mother as a daughter can," she explains. "If I were a boy I don't think I could feel as Mama feels or see things as she sees them." I doubt my grandmother would have questioned a boy's capacity to love his mother; whether she knew it then, she had married a man who, as an eight-year-old attending the funeral service for his recently deceased mother, leaped into her grave, refusing to be parted, a family legend I heard many times. Yet her words describe perfectly the matrilineal cycle of care she drew me into as a child when she ironed and sang and reminisced as the stitches on my forehead healed and I listened. The salve for our wounds. The source of my commitment to writing women's lives: I wanted to enable readers to feel and see things as my female subjects felt and saw them.

———

MY SISTER PHONES from her home in eastern Oregon: Have I ever seen Mom's self-portrait? She's been clearing out her attic; a portfolio of our mother's unframed paintings my sister stashed away decades ago, after we divided our mom's belongings, turned up. My sister scans the image and sends it to me, and it is like nothing I've seen before.

The painting is monochrome—blacks, grays, white—and the perspective intentionally distorted, but it's my mother seated at a table with a stick of charcoal or a pencil in her hand, musing over a blank sheet of paper. On a smaller adjacent table rest objects the college-girl artist may have been assigned to draw: plaster casts of two hands crossed, a winding length of rope. The image seems to be all about hands—the sketching hand is at the center of the painting—and I notice instantly that my mother has pictured herself right-handed. Could she have been copying her reflection in a mirror, resulting in a reverse image? No, her hair is parted correctly on the right. The choice seems deliberate. The more prominent of the plaster casts is a left hand, appearing at first glance to be a severed limb, tangled somehow in the twisting rope. It's tempting to take this early self-representation as an omen: a sign that already she'd wanted her life to be otherwise.

And perhaps she had. The artist, or writer, must step outside the frame to see her subject, to find its shape or imagine a new one. She'd used her despised yet precious left hand to sketch a different self—perhaps a more confident one, prepared to step outside the bounds of convention and choose to be an artist.

At first what I found in my mother's archive made me angry. Unlike Sophia Peabody, she had training as well as talent. I'd known that the celebrated California artist Richard Diebenkorn was a classmate of my mother's at UC Berkeley. Now I learned they'd exhibited together in a juried show of watercolors at the San Francisco Museum of Art (now SFMOMA) in 1946. Neither of them took a blue ribbon, but a review clipped from the *San Francisco Chronicle* singled out my mother's landscape, *Crystal Range*, selected for the next year's show, as deserving. They shared mentors—the professors Eugen Neuhaus and Worth Ryder, who'd brought one of his own teachers, Hans Hofmann, the guiding light of the abstract expressionists, to America in the early 1930s. These were the men my mother turned to for recommendations when she applied for a $1,200 Albert Bender fellowship in 1947.

She didn't get it—by then she'd married and was living on the East Coast, supporting herself and my grad student father in a job with the City of Cambridge Planning Department that paid a dollar an hour for a six-day week. The fellowship would have allowed her to cut back her work hours and given her "more free time to paint," she wrote to her mother, instructing her on how to submit a portfolio of eight paintings she'd left behind in California. Still, even without the fellowship, Elva Spiess Marshall found time to complete a handful of new landscapes, working from memory and photographs, to assemble a solo show of twenty-one

"Watercolors, Ink Drawings, Gouache, Tempera, Paintings" at the DeCordova Museum in suburban Boston in 1951. As she'd written to her parents in the early months of her marriage, when her alarmingly temperamental husband came close to "flunking out with finality," threatening their future plans: "I am not accustomed to giving up."

Nine months after the DeCordova show, my brother was born and my parents moved back to California. I was born in 1954 and my sister in 1955. My mother's last painting to earn recognition was displayed in a shopping plaza in Palo Alto in 1959. We moved to Pasadena in 1960, and her easel stayed folded up in the garage; I never saw her battered green paint box open.

I was angry at Richard Diebenkorn for the mix of factors, amounting to male privilege, that kept him at his easel developing his genius; he'd received the Bender fellowship the year before my mother applied, a significant turning point in his early career, enabling him to expand his craft and widen his circle of associations in the art world while his wife tended their two children. I was angry at the eminent Berkeley professors who didn't answer my mother's requests for letters of recommendation, forcing her to rely on endorsements from her architecture instructor and the family minister. Were they busy cultivating the talent of their male students, Diebenkorn included, whose numbers had swelled dramatically under the G.I. Bill in the two years since she graduated? Women, especially married women, were expected to step back. At work her requests for a raise were refused by the city manager, first because she "dressed in a California style" and then because "he didn't think he could give a raise to a housewife," she wrote to her mother.

Above all, I was angry at my father for messing up time and

again. Yet my mother's artist friends from college, whose names I'd heard so often as a child and found again in her letters—Edith, Mary Kay, Michal—had married successful professionals and still hadn't achieved significant acclaim. They'd let the careers of their husbands—a Stanford music professor, a biochemist, a renowned San Francisco gallery owner—take precedence. But I was forgetting the lesson I'd learned: do not judge a woman, even a woman of ambition and capability, by her accomplishments.

I study my mother's gorgeous, inventive landscapes on the walls of my apartment and see that all those signed "Elva Spiess" are dated 1946. Her wedding was in June of that year. Did love for the flawed man who became my father give her the energy and inspiration to paint at peak capacity, even while holding down her first full-time job after college? Of course she married him.

A different portrait of my mother forms in my mind's eye, one of the maturing woman whose words in weekly letters I've been reading. Her left-handed life unfurls: the "to-do" she instigated at the personnel office in Cambridge to finally get her raise; the stoic self-exhortation "Dejection serves no purpose" two decades later, after another of my father's work failures; and, through it all, the everyday details of my childhood and my siblings', in school and out. She's the mom I knew, yet whose inner life had, until now, like those of my biographical subjects, awaited my discovery.

She's seated beside a mountain path, sketchbook open in her lap, pencil flying as her family pauses to rest on a hike. The page is no longer blank.

EPILOGUE: SKYLIGHT

*I*N MAY 2023 I TRAVELED to New York City for the annual biographers conference I'd been attending four years earlier on the weekend Scott died. The conference had been held virtually each year since 2020, due to COVID, and I hadn't been sure I'd want to return when the group reconvened in person. I would never forget the four hours spent on an Acela train to Boston late in the day on May 19, 2019, as my texts to Scott went unanswered. This had happened before when I traveled, and Scott always scolded me for my concern—he'd forgotten to charge his phone or muted the ringer. I tried not to worry. But this day was different. The dark windows of our apartment when my taxi pulled up, the morning newspaper resting uncollected in its plastic sleeve on the doormat, told me so.

Four hours . . . four years. Time contracts and expands for the bereaved. The freshness of loss doesn't fade; years pass in an instant, reduced to a single reference point. Then and now come to have the same meaning: the beloved is gone. But the rhythms of life continue above the thrum of mourning. We look up and find a way back in.

I returned to the conference, then skipped out on a Saturday afternoon for a show of Georgia O'Keeffe watercolors at the Museum of Modern Art only to find the rooms impossibly crowded with O'Keeffe groupies. I fled up an escalator to the permanent collection. Turning into a small gallery that served as entrance to the broad exhibition space beyond, I noticed Andrew Wyeth's *Christina's World* filling the wall to my right, but scarcely glanced at the familiar painting. The image straight ahead, the focal point from the doorway, caught my attention instead. Was I looking at party streamers, or tie-dyed strips of fabric drying on a clothesline, blown by the wind? Moving closer I could make out a precise geometry: lines of black ironwork defined long rectangles of a luminous blue, six over six, with two panels open to the sun. A window. The label gave a confirming title, *Skylight*. The painter and date of composition: Loren MacIver, 1948.

Now I was cast back to another past, one I knew well, although I hadn't lived it. Loren MacIver had been one of Elizabeth Bishop's closest friends, possibly a lover. MacIver had been better known than Bishop in the early days of their friendship, her "renown" as a woman artist second only to O'Keeffe's, according to one critic; but that began to change in 1946 with the publication of Bishop's first book, a critical success, followed by a second collection ten years later, which won the Pulitzer. The women of abstract expressionism—Frankenthaler, Krasner, Mitchell, Hartigan—outpaced MacIver in the 1950s and '60s. Yet here was MacIver's *Skylight*, a vibrant, half-abstract masterpiece, given its own wall in a room hung with just four paintings, keeping company with the iconic *Christina's World* and a work called simply *Painting* by Willem de Kooning.

From my research into Elizabeth Bishop's life, I knew that skylight, too, and the tragic events that took place beneath it. Judging from the date, this had to be the cherished window that illuminated the top-floor studio in the apartment MacIver and her husband, the poet Lloyd Frankenberg, occupied at 61 Perry Street in Greenwich Village starting in 1942. Bishop sat for her portrait there that fall. Twenty-five years later, in 1967, Bishop spent a summer at Perry Street while MacIver and Frankenberg were in Paris, taking refuge from her increasingly stormy relationship with Lota de Macedo Soares in Brazil. Soares arrived from Rio on short notice in September, hoping to reconcile, but severely depressed; on her first night in the apartment, whether by accident or intention, Soares overdosed on Valium and did not survive. Nearly broken by Soares's death, Bishop nevertheless considered Frankenberg's suicide seven years later a "wise decision." Married in 1929 at ages twenty and twenty-two, MacIver and Frankenberg had their own problems. By the 1970s, Frankenberg suffered from a persistent mania, which repeated hospitalizations could not cure. He, too, overdosed, on sleeping pills, and died at 61 Perry Street in 1975.

But *Skylight* was still here and, with its azure panes, suggesting nothing tragic: a relic of a time when Bishop lived nearby in an apartment on King Street, where the three friends once dozed off together in bed after a night at the theater. That same year, 1947, was when Bishop first met Soares at a party in the 61 Perry Street apartment, and though she was initially attracted to Soares's partner, the dancer Mary Morse, the introduction led to an invitation to visit the couple at Soares's mountainside retreat in Brazil. By the time Bishop followed up on the offer, four years afterward in late 1951, Morse and Soares were living separately; Bishop moved in with Soares for what would be the happiest and most productive decade of her life.

"My wish is to make something permanent out of the transitory," MacIver wrote in an artist's statement composed for a MoMA group show, *Fourteen Americans,* in 1946, the year after her first solo show, at the Baltimore Museum of Art. When I returned home from New York City, I found an article on MacIver by Jenni Schlossman in *Woman's Art Journal,* which set the quotation in context. MacIver was one of three female artists in the MoMA show, now thought to have helped usher in the age of abstract expressionism, although MacIver and the two other women, I. Rice Pereira and Honoré Sharrer, never joined the club. Also selected for the show by MoMA's tastemaking curator Dorothy Miller were works by Arshile Gorky, Robert Motherwell, Isamu Noguchi, and Saul Steinberg. MacIver designed the catalog's cover, and when I located the publication online I felt a zing of recognition: there was the skylight's six-over-six pattern, rendered this time in solid white rectangles, holding the center of the page amid a swirl of sky blue and wispy white. Was MacIver warming up for the painting she would complete two years later?

I read more of MacIver's words: "Certain moments have the gift of revealing the past and foretelling the future. It is these moments that I hope to catch." Her paintings, she wrote, derive from "simple things"—the show included MacIver's *The Sidewalk, Hopscotch, Red Votive Lights, Ashcan,* and *Puddle*—which "lead the eye by various manipulations of colors, objects and tensions toward transformation and a reward." I was reminded of Bishop's pithy description of how a poem is made, although for her the process seemed to work in reverse, beginning with "a mystery and a surprise," followed by "a great deal of hard work" with the mechanics of formal verse. I thought, too, of how Bishop had resisted the gravitational pull of the soul-baring confessional poets, led by her friend Robert Lowell, in favor of a visual vocabulary of creatures and things whose presence in her poems leads to epiphany: a "tremendous fish" hooked and then set free in a "rainbow" swirl of motor oil and seawater; an armadillo's eyes caught in a car's headlights; the almanac, Little Marvel stove, and iron kettle that offer material comfort to an abandoned child and her weeping grandmother in "Sestina"; a she-moose that steps out of the Maine woods to halt a bus loaded with sleepy travelers, prompting the poet among them to ask, "Why, why do we feel / (we all feel) this sweet / sensation of joy?"

I learned that MacIver, who lived at 61 Perry Street until her death in 1998 at age eighty-nine, had painted the skylight again in 1985. In her *Skylight Storm*, the window is set askew, its edges hazy and its upper right corner lost from view. The colors aren't conventionally stormy—rather, pastel pinks and oranges, as if the sky had cleared at sunset. Three tiny smudged silhouettes of birds soar above, black against the sky. Two of the skylight's panes are cracked in half, one fracture giving its glass rectangle the appearance of a saddened face. Could the bisected panes mark the two suicides at 61 Perry Street? Might the three birds in flight recall the friendship of MacIver, Frankenberg, and Bishop—or picture the trio united again, one day, in death? More likely, MacIver just painted what she saw.

Still, what better "simple thing" than a window to capture the sense of simultaneously looking back to the past and ahead to the future that was MacIver's stated aim? In each iteration of the skylight pattern MacIver had indeed made the transitory permanent—or at least composed an image that outlasted its creator. Now I wanted to find out whether the skylight itself was still there.

On my next trip to New York City, I took the subway to Fourteenth Street and climbed the staircase to a Greenwich Village vastly different from the neighborhood Bishop had known in the 1940s and '60s, or MacIver had inhabited during her last decade, the 1990s. Past the restaurants with COVID-era sidewalk seating and a walk-up corner coffee bar (no indoor seating whatsoever), I found the quiet block of Perry Street where MacIver's narrow two-and-a-half-story house sits now between two tall apartment buildings, across the street from a row of town houses, its flat Federal-period brick facade a miracle of random urban preservation. MacIver lived in the top apartment, I knew not only from the skylight paintings, but from Bishop's report in a letter to MacIver and Frankenberg that the aroma of the downstairs tenant's coffee floated up through the bedroom floor each morning to wake her at 5:00 a.m. A long single gable with four south-facing windows raised the roofline, pulling sunshine into the loft where MacIver had painted. But that wasn't the skylight. As it turned out, I might have stayed home to find it: the Google Earth app on my iPhone obliged, landing its red thumbtack on the building's roof, enabling me to look down, virtually, on the same skylight through which MacIver, Frankenberg, Soares, and Bishop had once looked up.

But I was glad I'd made the trip. As I stood on the sidewalk across from 61 Perry Street, trying to make out a skylight and failing, I realized I was practicing biography again: hunting up obscure publications, tracking down letters, following my quarry to her lair. Would I write more about MacIver—plumb the mystery of the rise, fall, and seeming resurgence of her acclaim? I didn't know. But the desire was back. My season of introspection was receding, and once again I was eager to learn what I could from others: how to live, how not to live, what it means to live.

We are all biographers from childhood. Life is short, the ancient doctor Hippocrates warned, and art is long: the pursuit of a craft, and the lasting creation itself. So, too, is the art we make of lives. It was time to start in again.

ACKNOWLEDGMENTS

FEW WRITERS CAN LOOK BACK on a career spanning four decades and find they have only one literary agent and one editor to thank for shepherding them through it all. I am one such lucky author. Katinka Matson of Brockman Inc. believed in my biographies (and in me) from the start, and Deanne Urmy—of Houghton Mifflin, then Houghton Mifflin Harcourt, and finally HarperCollins's Mariner Books—stepped in as a new editor when *The Peabody Sisters* arrived at HMCo in 2004 after a slow gestation and oversaw its ultimate, blessed arrival in the world. She has treated every manuscript I've turned in since with equal care, offering astute guidance page by page and moral support whenever needed.

I am grateful to a veritable convoy of scholars, archivists, and curators, some of them cherished colleagues, who answered my questions or told me where to look for answers as I researched the essays of *After Lives:* Tish Hopkins, Sleepy Hollow Cemetery,

Concord, Massachusetts; Meg L. Winslow, Curator of Historical Collections and Archives, Mount Auburn Cemetery; Anne Bentley, Peter Drummey, Brenda Lawson, and Mary Yacovone, Massachusetts Historical Society; Amy Hietala, Old Sturbridge Village; Carla M. Lillvik, Special Collections, Monroe C. Gutman Library, Harvard Graduate School of Education; Melissa Carr, Masterwork Conservation; Tamar Brown, Jennifer Fauxsmith, and Sarah Hutcheon, Arthur and Elizabeth Schlesinger Library on the History of Women in America; Lydia Mullin, Department of Painting and Sculpture, Museum of Modern Art; Gary Wolf, architect; Dean Rogers, Archives and Special Collections Library, Vassar College. For assistance with research and the intricacies of publication: Laura Selene Rockefeller and Sherry A. Wells, Neil Giordano, Lisa Glover, Anna Morrison, Nancy Tan, Jessica Vestuto, and Megan Wilson.

For sharing insights, memories, travels, and research, I am indebted to Susan Abele, Gail Banks, Keiko Beppu, Monica Bethe, Kent Bicknell, Roger Bockrath, the late Supratik Bose, Don Clark, Alison Hawthorne Deming, Helen Deese, Bonnie Lee Grad, George Harpole, Yoshiko Ito, Shoko Itoh, Richard Kopley, Etta Madden, Thom Mayne, George Miller, Mari and Naoyuki Mizuno, Aiko Moroto, Yuri and Erisa Nagira, Karin Stanford, Christopher Alan Sutton, Masako Takeda, Dennis Wun, and Cloe Mayes Yocum.

Longtime friends and the editors of the publications in which some of the essays first appeared helped me find my way in the new form, talking through problems and reading drafts: Anne Gray Fischer, Rebecca Goldstein, David Haglund, Susan Holman, Pico Iyer, Mary C. Kelley, Jeff Mayersohn, Emily McKeage, Diane McWhorter, Kim Phillips-Fein, Stacy Schiff, Grace Shulman,

Christina Thompson, Heather Treseler, Susan Ware, and Joan Wickersham. The members of my biographers group gave the unstinting support that has kept us together since the 1980s: Joyce Antler, Frances Malino, Susan Quinn, Judith Tick, Roberta Wollons, and the late Lois Palken Rudnick. The women of my Dana-Farber Cancer Institute–founded bereavement group, Gina Cass, Mary Coogan, Beverley Daniel, Diane Heefner, Marilyn Rand, Paige Tobin, and Margo Walsh, shared mourning and celebration nearly every week since January 2020. And I could have done nothing without my family: in particular my sister, Amy Marshall; cousins Kathy Dallaire, Mary Liz DeJong, Lanette MacLeod, Peter Marshall, Helen Spiess Shamble, and Peggy DeLigio Spiess; and dearest daughters, Sara Sedgwick Brown and Josephine Sedgwick. These institutions offered sustenance and became family: Emerson College, the Bogliasco Foundation, T. S. Eliot House, and distant, but ever present in memory, Kyoto University.

Memory is inherently subjective, as biographers learn early in their work. My gratitude extends as well to anyone who might have "been there" during the events recounted from memory in this book and who may recall things differently. Your forbearance is a gift.

SOURCES

INTRODUCTION: VITAL DOCUMENTS

Bishop, Elizabeth. Passports. Elizabeth Bishop Papers, f.120.12–17, Archives and Special Collections Library, Vassar College.

Bradford, Gamaliel. "Confessions of a Biographer." In *Wives*, 3–14. New York: Harper & Brothers, 1925.

Edel, Leon. *Writing Lives: Principia Biographica*. New York: W. W. Norton, 1985.

Kendall, Paul Murray. *The Art of Biography*. New York: W. W. Norton, 1965.

AFTER LIVES

Abele, Susan D. "Ada Shepard and Her Pocket Sketchbooks, Florence 1858." *Nathaniel Hawthorne Review* 39, no. 1 (Spring 2013): 1–34.

Bonham, Valerie. *A Place in Life: The Clewer House of Mercy*,

1849–83. V. Bonham and the Community of St. John Baptist, 1992.

Brewster, Anne Hampton. Journal entry, March 28, 1872. Anne Hampton Brewster papers, Library Company of Philadelphia.

Corkran, Henriette. *Celebrities and I*. London: Hutchinson, 1902.

Culkin, Kate. "The Education of Ellen Tucker Emerson." *New England Quarterly* 93, no. 1 (March 2020): 74–100.

Ellis, Allison. "Ralph Waldo Emerson's Grave Encounters." *Ploughshares Longform* (blog), March 25, 2021. https://blog .pshares.org/ralph-waldo-emersons-grave-encounters/.

Emerson, Ralph Waldo. *The Journals and Miscellaneous Notebooks of Ralph Waldo Emerson*. Vol. 3, 1826–1832, edited by William H. Gilman and Alfred R. Ferguson. Cambridge, MA: Harvard University Press, 1963.

Emerson, Ralph Waldo. *The Journals and Miscellaneous Notebooks of Ralph Waldo Emerson*. Vol. 12, 1835–1862, edited by Linda Allardt. Cambridge, MA: Harvard University Press, 1976.

Emerson, Ralph Waldo. *The Journals and Miscellaneous Notebooks of Ralph Waldo Emerson*. Vol. 14, 1854–1861, edited by Susan Sutton Smith and Harrison Hayford. Cambridge, MA: Harvard University Press, 1978.

Emerson, Ralph Waldo. *The Journals and Miscellaneous Notebooks of Ralph Waldo Emerson*. Vol. 16, 1866–1882, edited by Ronald A. Bosco and Glen M. Johnson. Cambridge, MA: Harvard University Press, 1982.

Emerson, Ralph Waldo, ed. *Parnassus*. Boston and New York: Houghton Mifflin, 1874.

Evans, Constantine. "Hawthorne's Contribution to *Weal-reaf.*"
    Nathaniel Hawthorne Review 29, no. 1 (Spring 2003): 46–65.
Gates, Barbara. *Victorian Suicide: Mad Crimes and Sad Histories.*
    Princeton, NJ: Princeton University Press, 1988.
Hardwick, Elizabeth. *The Uncollected Essays of Elizabeth
    Hardwick.* Edited by Alex Andriesse. New York: New York
    Review Books, 2022.
Hawksley, Lucinda. *Bitten by Witch Fever: Wallpaper and Arsenic
    in the Victorian Home.* London: Thames & Hudson, 2016.
Hawthorne, Julian. *The Memoirs of Julian Hawthorne.* Edited by
    Edith Garrigues Hawthorne. New York: Macmillan, 1938.
Hawthorne, Julian. *Nathaniel Hawthorne and His Wife: A
    Biography.* Boston: Houghton Mifflin, 1897.
Hawthorne, Nathaniel. *The American Notebooks.* Edited by
    Claude M. Simpson. Columbus: Ohio State University
    Press, 1972.
Hawthorne, Nathaniel. *The Letters: 1843–1853.* Centenary ed.,
    vol. 16, edited by Thomas Woodson, L. Neal Smith, and
    Norman Holmes Pearson. Columbus: Ohio State University
    Press, 1985.
Hawthorne, Nathaniel. *The Letters: 1857–1864.* Centenary ed.,
    vol. 18, edited by Thomas Woodson, James A. Rubino, L. Neal
    Smith, and Norman Holmes Pearson. Columbus: Ohio State
    University Press, 1987.
Hawthorne, Nathaniel. *The Scarlet Letter.* (various editions)
Hawthorne, Nathaniel. *Tales and Sketches.* New York: Library
    of America, 1982.
Herbert, T. Walter. *Dearest Beloved: The Hawthornes and the
    Making of the Middle-Class Family.* Berkeley: University of
    California Press, 1993.

Higginson, Thomas Wentworth. *The Letters and Journals of Thomas Wentworth Higginson, 1846–1906.* Edited by Mary Thacher Higginson. Boston: Houghton Mifflin, 1921.

Higginson, Thomas Wentworth. *Part of a Man's Life.* Boston: Houghton Mifflin, 1905.

Hull, Raymona. "Una Hawthorne: A Biographical Sketch." *Nathaniel Hawthorne Journal* 6 (1976): 87–119.

Loggins, Vernon. *The Hawthornes: The Story of Seven Generations of an American Family.* New York: Columbia University Press, 1951.

Madden, Etta M. *Engaging Italy: American Women's Utopian Visions and Transnational Networks.* Albany: State University of New York Press, 2022.

Marks, Patricia. "Una Hawthorne's 'House for Orphans Tiny.'" *Emerson Society Quarterly* 25, no. 1 (1979): 17–19.

Marshall, Megan. *The Peabody Sisters: Three Women Who Ignited American Romanticism.* Boston: Houghton Mifflin, 2005.

Marshall, Megan. "Sophia's Crimson Hand." *Nathaniel Hawthorne Review* 37, no. 2 (Fall 2011): 36–46.

Mays, James O'Donald. *Mr. Hawthorne Goes to England: The Adventures of a Reluctant Consul.* Ringwood, Hampshire, UK: New Forest Leaves, 1983.

"Miss Una Hawthorne." *South London Chronicle,* September 15, 1877.

Peabody, Elizabeth Palmer. Letter to Mary Channing Eustis, October 28, 1876. Collection of Kent Bicknell.

Peabody, Nathaniel Cranch. Peabody family genealogical notes, entry on Una Hawthorne, typescript. Antiochiana collection, Antioch College Library.

Richardson, Robert D., Jr. *Emerson: The Mind on Fire*. Berkeley: University of California Press, 1995.

Ross, John J. *Shakespeare's Tremor and Orwell's Cough: Diagnosing the Medical Groans and Last Gasps of Ten Great Writers*. New York: St. Martin's Press, 2012.

Shefer, Elaine. "Deverell, Rossetti, Siddal, and 'The Bird in the Cage.'" *Art Bulletin* 67, no. 3 (September 1985): 437–48.

Shepard, Ada. Letter to Clay Badger, October 16, 1857, typescript. Beinecke Rare Book and Manuscript Library, Yale University.

"St. Andrew's Cottage, Clewer, Near Windsor / Temporary Home and House of Rest for Ladies of Small Means, Not Invalids." Berkshire Records Office Collection.

"Suicide of a Son of Herman Melville." *Daily Alta California*, October 2, 1867.

von Mehren, Joan. "Margaret Fuller, the Marchese Giovanni Ossoli, and the Marriage Question: Considering the Research of Dr. Roberto Colzi." *Resources for American Literary Study* 30, no. 1 (2005): 104–43.

THE SECOND MAN IN THE FRONT ROW

Alam, Fakrul, and Radha Chakravarty. *The Essential Tagore*. Cambridge, MA: Harvard University Press, 2011.

Beatty, Jack. *The Lost History of 1914: Reconsidering the Year the Great War Began*. New York: Walker, 2012.

Brooke, Rupert. *Letters from America*. 1916. New York: Beaufort Books, 1988.

Carroll, Andrew. *My Fellow Soldiers: General John Pershing and the Americans Who Helped Win the Great War*. New York: Penguin Press, 2017.

Emmerson, Charles. *1913: In Search of the World Before the Great War*. New York: PublicAffairs, 2013.

Marshall, Elizabeth Metcalf. Diary June–September 1917. Marshall-Spiess family papers, Arthur and Elizabeth Schlesinger Library on the History of Women in America, Radcliffe Institute for Advanced Study at Harvard University.

Marshall, Joe T. Papers. Harvard University Archives.

Metcalf family. Papers. Burton Historical Collection, Detroit Public Library.

Tagore, Rabindranath. *My Life in My Words*. New Delhi: Penguin, 2006.

Tagore, Rabindranath. *Sādhanā: The Realisation of Life*. New York: Macmillan, 1914.

FREE FOR A WHILE

Abbott, Carl. "Pasadena on Her Mind: Octavia E. Butler Reimagines Her Hometown." *Los Angeles Review of Books,* February 2, 2019.

Berger, Dan. *Captive Nation: Black Prison Organizing in the Civil Rights Era*. Chapel Hill: University of North Carolina Press, 2014.

Browne, Lee F. Interview by Shirley K. Cohen, June 14, 1999. Archives, California Institute of Technology.

Butler, Octavia. *Parable of the Sower*. New York: Grand Central Publishing, 2019.

Butler, Octavia. *Parable of the Talents*. New York: Grand Central Publishing, 2019.

Davis, Angela. *An Autobiography*. New York: Random House, 1974.

Davis, Mike, and Jon Wiener. *Set the Night on Fire: L.A. in the Sixties*. London: Verso, 2020.

"Dr. Martin Luther King Jr.'s Three Visits to Pasadena Were Indelible Moments." *Pasadena Now,* January 15, 2018. https://www.pasadenanow.com/main/martin-luther -kings-three-visits-to-pasadena-left-an-indelible-mark.

Francis, Consuela, ed. *Conversations with Octavia Butler.* Jackson: University Press of Mississippi, 2010.

"The Funeral of Jonathan Jackson and William Christmas." KPFA, August 15, 1970. Pacifica Radio Archives, American Archive of Public Broadcasting, http://americanarchive .org/catalog/cpb-aacip-28-7p8tb0z23q.

Gomez, Melissa. "After Admitting Founder's Eugenics Past, Caltech Honors a Diversity of Campus Figures." *Los Angeles Times,* November 10, 2021.

Hormann, Matt. "Night of Terror." *Pasadena Weekly,* November 5, 2015.

Houlemard, Michael. Interview by Karin L. Stanford, July 27, 2020. Tom & Ethel Bradley Center, California State University Northridge.

Hudson, Lynn M. *West of Jim Crow: The Fight Against California's Color Line.* Urbana: University of Illinois Press, 2020.

Jackson, George L. *Blood in My Eye.* Baltimore, MD: Black Classic Press, 1990.

Jackson, George L. *Soledad Brother: The Prison Letters of George Jackson.* New York: Bantam, 1970.

Jackson, Georgia. Interview by *Black Journal.* Episode 32, "Justice?" Aired April 16, 1971, NET Division, Educational Broadcasting Corporation. "The 50th Anniversary of the

August 7th Marin County Courthouse Rebellion," Freedom
Archives, https://freedomarchives.org/projects/the-50th
-anniversary-of-the-august-7th-marin-county-courthouse
-rebellion/.

Jackson, Jonathan. "Faculty Seeks Award." *Iskra,* April 1, 1970.

Jackson, Jonathan. "Jackson Article Reprinted." *Iskra,* January
5, 1971.

Jackson, Jonathan. "Racist Educational Structure Attacked."
Iskra, April 1, 1970.

Jackson, Jonathan Peter. "Bio." Jonathan Peter Jackson,
https://www.jonathanpeterjackson.com/biography.

Jackson v. Pasadena City School Dist., June 27, 1963. Justia,
https://law.justia.com/cases/california/supreme-
court/2d/59/876.html.

Jones, Denise Houlemard. Interview by Karin L. Stanford,
October 24, 2020. Tom & Ethel Bradley Center, California
State University Northridge.

Kendi, Ibram X. *Stamped from the Beginning: The Definitive
History of Racist Ideas in America.* New York: Bold Type
Books, 2016.

"Last Act." *Pagan Writes,* June 15, 1971.

"Lee Browne." *The Month at Caltech,* 1970. California
Institute of Technology, https://resolver.caltech.edu
/CaltechES:34.1.themonth.

"Lee Browne Interview." *Iskra,* February 25, 1970.

"Lee Franke Browne." Obituary, n.d. Archives, California
Institute of Technology.

Lester, Julius. "Black Rage to Live." *New York Times,*
November 22, 1970.

Liberatore, Paul. *The Road to Hell: The True Story of George Jackson, Stephen Bingham, and the San Quentin Massacre.* New York: Atlantic Monthly Press, 1996.

Lowery, Lucy. "Slain Pasadenan's Obsession Related." *Pasadena Star-News,* August 19, 1970.

Mitford, Jessica. "A Talk with George Jackson." *New York Times Book Review,* June 13, 1971.

Pasadena City Board of Education et al., petitioners, v. Nancy Anne Spangler et al. U.S. Supreme Court decision, June 28, 1976. Legal Information Institute, Cornell Law School, https://www.law.cornell.edu/supremecourt/text/427/424.

Stuart, Carolyn. "Public Housing in California." SAH Archipedia, Society of American Historians. https://sah-archipedia.org/essays/CA-01-ART-03.

Thompson, Heather Ann. *Blood in the Water: The Attica Prison Uprising of 1971 and Its Legacy.* New York: Vintage, 2016.

Turpin, Dick. "Pasadena Pepper Redevelopment Project: Co-op Venture First in Country." *Los Angeles Times,* January 4, 1970.

Williams, Ben. "Marin County Courthouse Shootout." KPIX Eyewitness News, August 7, 1970. Bay Area Television Archive, San Francisco State University, https://diva.sfsu.edu/collections/sfbatv/bundles/190039.

Yee, Min S. *The Melancholy History of Soledad Prison: In Which a Utopian Scheme Turns Bedlam.* New York: Harper's Magazine Press, 1973.

Zack, Michele. *Altadena: Between Wilderness and City.* Altadena, CA: Altadena Historical Society, 2004.

THESE USELESS THINGS

Works cited

Auslander, Leora. "Beyond Words." *American Historical Review* 110, no. 4 (October 2005): 1015–45.

Carpenter, Dolores Bird, ed. *The Selected Letters of Lidian Jackson Emerson*. Columbia: University of Missouri Press, 1987.

Classified Telephone Directory for Los Angeles, June 1936. U.S. Telephone Directory Collection, Library of Congress.

Marshall, Megan. *The Peabody Sisters: Three Women Who Ignited American Romanticism*. Boston: Houghton Mifflin, 2005.

Peabody, Elizabeth P. Brookline diary entry, August 12, 1826. Quoted in Mary Van Wyck Church draft biography of Elizabeth Palmer Peabody, Massachusetts Historical Society.

Peabody, Elizabeth P. Letter to Sophia A. Peabody, August 23, 1825. Berg Collection, New York Public Library.

Peabody, Elizabeth P. Letter to Sophia A. Peabody, August 14, 1825 (really 1826). Peabody Family Papers, Sophia Smith Collection, Smith College.

Peabody, Mary T. *Primer of Reading and Drawing*. Boston: E. P. Peabody, 1841.

Prown, Jules David. *Art as Evidence: Writings on Art and Material Culture*. New Haven, CT: Yale University Press, 2001.

Richardson, Robert D. *Three Roads Back: How Emerson, Thoreau, and William James Responded to the Greatest Losses of Their Lives*. Princeton, NJ: Princeton University Press, 2023.

Thoreau, Henry David. *Walden*. (various editions)

Updike, John. *The Centaur*. New York: Knopf, 1964.

Updike, John. *Rabbit at Rest*. New York: Knopf, 1990.

Updike, John. *Rabbit Is Rich*. New York: Knopf, 1981.

Updike, John. *Rabbit Redux*. New York: Knopf, 1971.

Updike, John. *Rabbit, Run*. New York: Knopf, 1960.

Wyma, Mike. "The Day of the Digits: Postscript to the Prefix War." *Los Angeles Times,* October 20, 1988.

Works consulted

Brown, Bill. *A Sense of Things: The Object Matter of American Literature*. Chicago: University of Chicago Press, 2003.

Brown, Bill. "Thing Theory." *Critical Inquiry* 28, no. 1 (Autumn 2001): 1–22.

Carter, Sarah Anne. *Object Lessons: How Nineteenth-Century Americans Learned to Make Sense of the Material World*. New York: Oxford University Press, 2018.

Csikszentmihalyi, Mihaly, and Eugene Rochberg-Halton. *The Meaning of Things: Domestic Symbols and the Self.* Cambridge: Cambridge University Press, 1981.

Hannan, Leonie, and Sarah Longair. *History Through Material Culture*. Manchester: Manchester University Press, 2017.

Hicks, Dan, and Mary C. Beaudry, eds. *The Oxford Handbook of Material Culture Studies*. Oxford: Oxford University Press, 2010.

Hoskins, Janet. *Biographical Objects: How Things Tell the Stories of People's Lives*. New York: Routledge, 1998.

Masters, Nathan. "How Ice First Came to Frost-Free Los Angeles." *Lost LA,* November 18, 2015. https://www .pbssocal.org/shows/lost-la/how-ice-first-came-to-frost -free-los-angeles#:~:text=Ice%20first%20became%20 commercially%20available,and%20the%20USC%20 Digital%20Library.

Miller, Peter N. *Cultural Histories of the Material World*. Ann Arbor: University of Michigan Press, 2013.

Muensterberger, Werner. *Collecting: An Unruly Passion*. Princeton, NJ: Princeton University Press, 1994.

Seaburg, Carl, and Stanley Paterson. *The Ice King: Frederic Tudor and His Circle*. Edited by Alan Seaburg. Boston: Massachusetts Historical Society, 2003.

Ulrich, Laurel Thatcher, Ivan Gaskell, Sara J. Schechner, and Sarah Anne Carter. *Tangible Things: Making History Through Objects*. New York: Oxford University Press, 2015.

WITHOUT

Chōmei, Kamo no. "An Account of a Ten-Foot-Square Hut." Translated by Anthony Chambers. In *Traditional Japanese Literature: An Anthology, Beginnings to 1600*, edited by Haruo Shirane, 624–35. New York: Columbia University Press, 2007.

Chōmei, Kamo no. *Hojoki: Visions of a Torn World*. Translated by Yasuhiko Moriguchi and David Jenkins. Berkeley, CA: Stone Bridge Press, 1996.

Hawthorne, Nathaniel. *The Blithedale Romance*. (various editions)

Jauhar, Sandeep. *Heart: A History*. New York: Farrar, Straus and Giroux, 2018.

Peabody, Elizabeth Palmer, trans. "The Preaching of Buddha." *Dial* 4, no. 3 (January 1844): 391–401.

Thoreau, Henry David. *Walden*. (various editions)

LEFT-HANDED

"Area Art Club Show Winners." *Palo Alto Times*, May 30, 1959.

Coren, Stanley. *The Left-Hander Syndrome: The Causes and Consequences of Left-Handedness*. New York: Free Press, 1992.

de Kovel, Carolien, Amaia Carrión-Castillo, and Clyde Francks. "A Large-Scale Population Study of Early Life Factors Influencing Left-Handedness." *Scientific Reports* 9, no. 1 (January 24, 2019): 584.

Edwards, Betty. *Drawing on the Right Side of the Brain: A Course in Enhancing Creativity and Artistic Confidence*. 4th ed. New York: Jeremy P. Tarcher/Penguin, 2012.

Eleventh Annual Watercolor Exhibition: San Francisco Art Association, March 13 Through April 13, 1947. San Francisco: San Francisco Museum of Art, 1947.

"Fiskars' Scissors Celebrate 55th Anniversary—Do You Know How the Iconic Orange Color Was Invented?" Design Stories, April 13, 2022. https://www.finnishdesignshop.com/design-stories/classic/fiskars-scissors-celebrate-55th-anniversary.

Kushner, Howard I. *On the Other Hand: Left Hand, Right Brain, Mental Disorder, and History*. Baltimore, MD: Johns Hopkins University Press, 2017.

Marshall, Megan. *The Peabody Sisters: Three Women Who Ignited American Romanticism*. Boston: Houghton Mifflin, 2005.

Marshall-Spiess family papers. Arthur and Elizabeth Schlesinger Library on the History of Women in America, Radcliffe Institute for Advanced Study at Harvard University.

McManus, Chris. *Right Hand, Left Hand: The Origins of Asymmetry in Brains, Bodies, Atoms and Cultures*. Cambridge, MA: Harvard University Press, 2002.

Ocklenburg, Sebastian. "Left-Handedness and Neurodiversity: A Surprising Link." *Psychology Today*, December 18, 2022. https://www.psychologytoday.com/us/blog/the-asymmetric-brain/202212/left-handedness-and-neurodiversity-a-surprising-link.

Rawsthorn, Alice. "Reflections on a Soup Spoon." *New York Times*, May 11, 2012.

Searing, Linda. "The Big Number: Lefties Make Up About 10 Percent of the World." *Washington Post*, August 12, 2019.

Smits, Rik. *The Puzzle of Left-Handedness*. London: Reaktion Books, 2011.

Springer, Sally P., and Georg Deutsch. *Left Brain, Right Brain: Perspectives on Cognitive Neuroscience*. San Francisco: W. H. Freeman, 1981.

Stephens, Ransom. *The Left Brain Speaks, the Right Brain Laughs: A Look at the Neuroscience of Innovation & Creativity in Art, Science & Life*. New York: Viva Editions, 2016.

Tenth Annual Watercolor Exhibition: San Francisco Art Association, April 17th Through May 5th, 1946. San Francisco: San Francisco Museum of Art, 1946.

Wilson, Daniel. *The Right Hand: Left-Handedness*. New York: Macmillan, 1891.

EPILOGUE: SKYLIGHT

Bishop, Elizabeth. Letters to Ruth Foster, February 1947. Elizabeth Bishop Papers, f.118.33, Archives and Special Collections Library, Vassar College.

Bishop, Elizabeth. *One Art: Letters*. Edited by Robert Giroux. New York: Farrar, Straus and Giroux, 1994.

Butler, Sharon L. "Tracking Loren MacIver." *Brooklyn Rail*, March 2008. https://brooklynrail.org/2008/03/artseen /tracking.

Cotter, Holland. "Loren MacIver, 90, a Painter Known for Her Eclectic Style." *New York Times*, May 24, 1998.

Miller, Dorothy C., ed. *Fourteen Americans*. New York: Museum of Modern Art, 1946.

Miller, Tom. "A House Where Art Was Created—61 Perry Street." *Daytonian in Manhattan* (blog), May 23, 2013. https://daytoninmanhattan.blogspot.com/2013/05/a -house-where-art-was-created-no-61.html.

Schlossman, Jenni L. "Loren MacIver: Turning the Ordinary into the Extraordinary." *Woman's Art Journal* 21, no. 1 (Spring–Summer 2000): 11–16.

CREDITS

Lines from letter to Jonathan Jackson from George Jackson, September 9, 1969, excerpted from *Soledad Brother: The Prison Letters of George Jackson* by George Jackson, copyright © 1994 by Jonathan Jackson Jr. Used by permission of Chicago Review Press. All rights reserved.

ILLUSTRATION CREDITS

Una Hawthorne. Photograph courtesy of Rosary Hill Home, Archives, Dominican Sisters, Congregation of St. Rose of Lima.

Una Hawthorne, sketch by Julian Hawthorne. Courtesy of Hawthorne Family Papers, Bancroft Library, University of California, Berkeley.

"The last services for the first Americans to die in France," Bathelémont, France, November 14, 1917. WWI A.E.F. Photograph Collection, #4061, State Historical Society of Iowa, Special Collections, Iowa City.

Story hour, Pasadena Central Library, summer 1960. Courtesy of the author.

Carl Maston [architect], Pepper Tree redevelopment (Pasadena, Calif.), 1970. Photograph by Julius Shulman. © J. Paul Getty Trust. Getty Research Institute, Los Angeles (2004.R.10).

Ice pick. Photograph by Laura Wulf.

Signpost. Photograph by the author.

Architectural rendering of Kamo no Chōmei's hut by Shigekazu Kawashiro. Reprinted by permission of the artist.

Elva Spiess [Marshall] self-portrait. Courtesy of the author.